JOURNEY THROUGH

NATURE

JOURNEY THROUGH

NATURE

JIM FLEGG

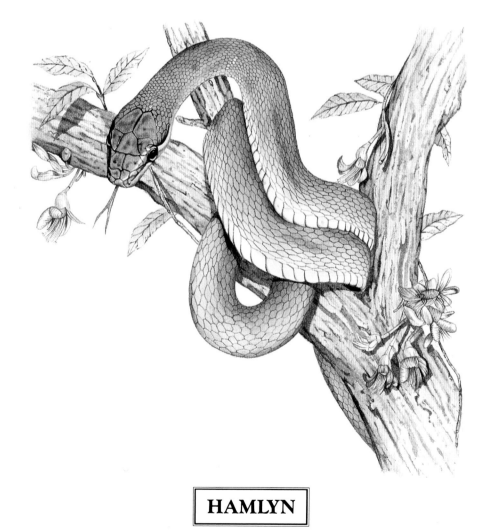

HAMLYN

Published in 1991 by
Hamlyn Children's Books,
part of Reed International Books,
Michelin House, 81 Fulham Road,
London SW3 6RB

ISBN 0 600 57116 5

Printed in Italy

CONTENTS

THE NATURAL WORLD

The natural world is divided into two kingdoms – plants and animals – put in that order because all life on earth depends ultimately on plants. Besides their own beauty, and fascinating diversity of shape, life style and colour, plants are important because they recycle atmospheric gases vital to life on earth, and provide the animal kingdom with its food. Plant-eating animals are called herbivores. Flesh-eating animals such as lions (called carnivores) eat herbivores such as antelopes and therefore they too depend on plants for food, at second hand.

This pattern is as true of microscopic life as it is of life on the African plains. In the sea, plant-plankton (or phytoplankton) is consumed by tiny animals, the zooplankton, which in turn are eaten by fish. These fish may be eaten by seabirds, or by larger fish. These in their turn are eaten by seals, which are the main prey of creatures such as killer whales or (in the Arctic) polar bears.

So, in each habitat, sea, forest, farm, or any other, a pyramid of life can be built up, with a wide range of plants at its base and a super-predator at its summit. All of these plants and animals have their place in the web of life that holds this structure together, and each is dependent in some way on the others. This is why the extinction of even one species of plant or animal matters, for each species is important not just for its own sake but because, if one strand in the web is broken, the whole structure (called an ecosystem) can be put at risk. Extinctions often occur because human interference or destruction upset the balance of nature, and this is why conservation is so important.

Plant Diversity

The range of plant life is amazing, from single-celled bacteria living for just a few hours to giant forest trees centuries old. Most plants are green, harnessing the sun's energy to help make their own food – and that of the animal kingdom. But not all: fungi cannot do this, and all must live off other substances as different as cheese and jam, and decaying plant material. Many fungi are parasites, drawing food from other plants and even animals. Some plants are predators, catching insects to provide chemicals missing in the soil. Some live largely underground, others scramble to reach the vital light. Some flower in spectacular

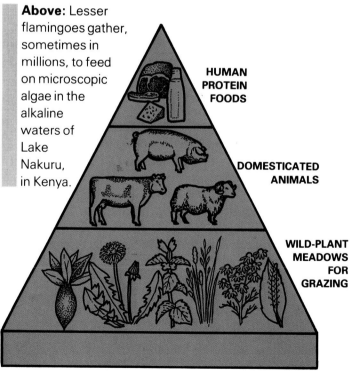

Above: Lesser flamingoes gather, sometimes in millions, to feed on microscopic algae in the alkaline waters of Lake Nakuru, in Kenya.

HUMAN PROTEIN FOODS

DOMESTICATED ANIMALS

WILD-PLANT MEADOWS FOR GRAZING

TOTAL LIVING SPECIES • OVER 1 MILLION INSECTS • 9,000 WORMS • 25,000 FISH

ways, while others send out runners or side shoots, rarely setting seed.

Animal Diversity

Animals are just as diverse in their size and life histories. The larger animals may seem to be the most interesting, but the vertebrates – animals with backbones – make up only 5 per cent of living animals. The remainder, the invertebrates, are equally fascinating. Some live at depths in the ocean that would crush an unprotected human diver to pulp, while one microscopic nematode worm lives its specialized life in old beer mats!

Because of their more active and complex lives, animals have far more sophisticated sensory systems than plants, and they use them to monitor all aspects of their environment. The ways in which they move about their environment are fascinatingly varied, and some of their travels unbelievable, covering half the globe and navigating with pinpoint accuracy. Both vegetarian and carnivore must find good food and recognize poisons, and distinguish friend from foe in their environment. Many exploit the benefits of living in herds or flocks, or breeding in colonies. Hunters must develop techniques of speed or stealth, and their prey must develop escape or defensive tactics.

Continuous Change

The history of the earth is one of ceaseless change. The processes in plants and animals of evolution and adaptation never stop, but are very slow. In most organisms little change will be detectable during a human lifetime – but we are observing the outcome of millions of years of evolution. All this variety of shape, structure, and way of life in the plant and animal kingdoms reflects the pressures of living in, and exploiting successfully, an ever-changing world, and makes a journey through nature so fascinating.

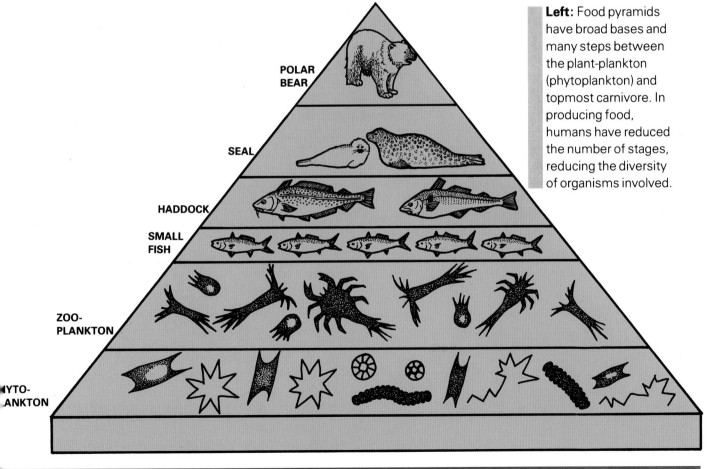

POLAR BEAR

SEAL

HADDOCK

SMALL FISH

ZOO-PLANKTON

PHYTO-PLANKTON

Left: Food pyramids have broad bases and many steps between the plant-plankton (phytoplankton) and topmost carnivore. In producing food, humans have reduced the number of stages, reducing the diversity of organisms involved.

3,000 AMPHIBIANS • 6,000 REPTILES • 9,000 BIRDS • 4,000 MAMMALS • 400,000 PLANTS

PAST AND FUTURE

Scientists think that the earth was formed about 5,000 million years ago from a fast-spinning mass of white-hot gases and dust, which gradually condensed into a sphere of molten rock. As it cooled, a rock crust appeared, which broke up into several vast plates of rock floating on a molten core. Seas began to form, but everything was very different from today. We think that the atmosphere then was made up of the gases hydrogen, methane, ammonia and water vapour, all except the last of which are poisonous to life. The molten interior erupted frequently as volcanoes, and electrical storms with lightning discharges were frequent.

Over millions of years, these immense chemical energies converted some of the simple organic chemicals present into larger, long-chain molecules bearing some similarity to life-building chemicals such as

Below: The fossil remains of plants and animals allow us to picture the earth's development.

Above right: Jellyfish are some of the earliest multi-celled creatures to be found in fossil form.

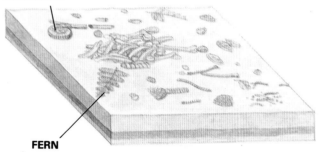

AMMONITE

FERN

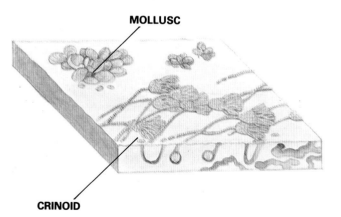

MOLLUSC

CRINOID

amino acids. Further action of these potent chemical forces on this "primordial soup" created proteins, carbohydrates and nucleic-acid chains. Gradually, the hostile atmosphere changed, the earth cooled still further, and life, the natural world as we know it, began.

First Life

We assume that life first appeared in the sea, probably in the form of ancestral single-celled algae and bacteria. Traces of such life can be found in rocks which geologists date as somewhere between 2,000 and 3,000 million years old. These traces of long-dead plants and animals – fossils – provide vital clues about the various steps in plant and animal evolution.

Unfortunately, fossils provide an incomplete story. Only sedimentary rocks, deposited as mud or silt in lakes or seas many millions of years ago, hold fossils, so there are obviously more fossils of creatures living in or near water than away from it. Some plants and animals, with tough fibres, hard shells or strong bones, fossilize better than others, but size is not always important. Chalk cliffs are formed from the skeletons of millions of microscopic diatoms, while coal seams are the compressed remains of swamp plants. The missing links are many, and tantalizing.

Slow Progress

The earliest stages of the evolution of plant and animal life were slow. Not until rocks dating from 600 million years ago do fossils become numerous, and then,

NEW ZEALAND LIZARD TUATARA FIRST SEEN ON EARTH 200 MILLION YEARS AGO

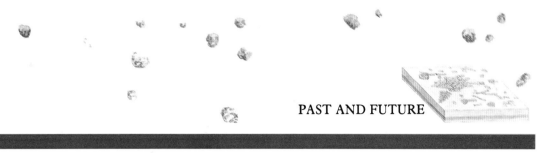

kingdom until 150 million years ago.

Early mammals appeared little more than 200 million years ago. Their evolution as warm-blooded animals, able to control their body temperature and thus not have their activity restrained by cold temperatures, gave them a competitive edge over the reptiles, an edge shared by birds, also warm-blooded, which appeared soon after. These two groups, with the insects, are the dominant land animals today, while the sea is the province still of fish.

Left: Safe from predators, the flightless cormorant has lost the power of flight.

amazingly, of marine creatures clearly recognizable as sea urchins. About 400 million years ago, an atmosphere containing vital oxygen developed. This allowed land plants to develop, first of all mosses, liverworts and ferns. By 200 million years ago, conifer forests were widespread, but not until just over 100 million years ago did flowering plants appear.

In the animal kingdom, fish dominated the world from about 450 million years ago until, 50 million years later, the first primitive amphibians struggled onto the land to exploit the oxygen just becoming available because of plant activity (p. 17). Winged insects also first appear in the fossil record at this time. About 350 million years ago saw the earliest reptiles, better adapted to life on dry land than the amphibians, which needed damp habitats and water in which to breed. Reptiles became steadily more numerous and more varied in size and habits, dominating the animal

Right: The earliest life forms developed in turbulent conditions.

AFRICAN FISH COELACANTH FIRST SEEN ON EARTH 250 MILLION YEARS AGO

THE LIVES OF ANIMALS

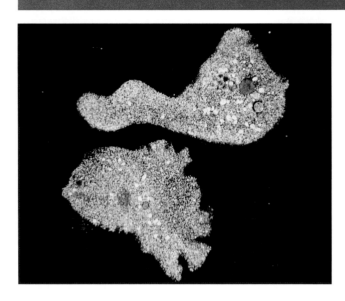

or juvenile stages. These may look like miniature versions of the adults (earthworms, aphids), or may be totally unlike their parents (caterpillars), often occupying a different habitat (crabs). Young grow steadily, shedding their skins at intervals in a process called moult. In some, caterpillars for example, a pupal stage follows, where a dramatic transformation takes place within a cocoon. The way caterpillar cells are reorganized to form the emerging moth or butterfly is still not fully understood.

In vertebrates, the animals with backbones, females are often recognizably distinct from males. In fish and amphibians, females release eggs with flimsy shells, provided with a yolk as food store for the developing embryo, while males wait nearby to release

To increase their numbers, the lowliest single-celled animals such as *Amoeba* may simply divide into two, but the general pattern of reproduction among invertebrate animals is for both male and female sex cells, sperm and ova (or eggs), to be produced. When these join in fertilization, a mixing of genetic material follows, and this creates minor variations in the offspring produced that make possible evolutionary "fine tuning". Sometimes major mutants may occur: most will be doomed, but on rare occasions mutants find opportunities to succeed in changing circumstances, and a new species may arise.

From the Egg

After fertilization, invertebrate eggs are often set free into their environment. Eggs hatch to liberate larval

Above left: Genetically identical twins, two new amoebas move apart after the division of their parent.

Below: A female African elephant strides swiftly towards its next huge meal. Its calf, just a few months old, trots at its heels.

BLUE WHALES WEIGH 2,000 kg AT BIRTH • QUEEN BEES LAY 1,500 EGGS A DAY

sperm into the water to fertilize them. Fish eggs develop into "fry", tiny replicas of their parents, but amphibian eggs hatch to produce a fish-shaped larva or tadpole, with fins and gills. These it loses later as it gradually turns into a small frog. In some fish, such as dogfish, males introduce their sperm into the females' oviduct (the tube running from the ovary to the outside world) using specially shaped fins. This is a safer way of being sure that her eggs are fertilized than releasing sperm into the sea.

Internal fertilization is the rule in reptiles and birds. Here, females lay eggs with a large yolk food store and a thick protective shell. These may be further protected by some form of nest, and in the case of birds guarded and warmed by parents. Reptiles usually abandon their eggs and young, while birds have very well-developed patterns of parental care (p. 52).

From the Womb

The most primitive mammals, spiny anteaters and

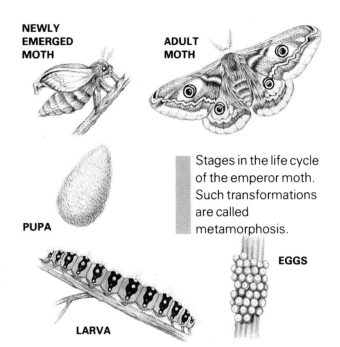

NEWLY EMERGED MOTH

ADULT MOTH

PUPA

Stages in the life cycle of the emperor moth. Such transformations are called metamorphosis.

EGGS

LARVA

duck-billed platypus, still lay eggs rather as reptiles do, but they are exceptions. The remaining mammals give birth to live babies following internal fertilization. The male uses a special organ called a penis to inject his sperm into the female's oviduct, up which the sperm swim to fertilize the eggs. The embryos (unborn babies) develop in the womb (or uterus), where they get food and oxygen from their mother's blood through the placenta, which clamps onto the uterus wall and transfers these vital necessities to the baby along the umbilical cord. The uterus itself is full of water, to cushion and protect the baby, so young mammals live underwater until they are born. For the first few days, traces of gills can be seen in many embryos, an evolutionary reminder of their fish ancestors.

Marsupials, the pouched animals characteristic of Australia, give birth to their young after only a few days or weeks in the uterus. In more advanced mammals, ranging from mice to whales, young live in their mother's uterus for a much greater part of their development. She gives birth to babies that are well enough developed to be left alone for periods while she searches for food. All mammal young grow swiftly on the rich milk provided by their mother from her special breasts or mammary glands.

OLDEST ELEPHANT 75 YEARS • ETRUSCAN SHREWS EAT 3 × OWN WEIGHT DAILY

HOW ANIMALS GROW

All animals face the same basic problems if they are to survive and flourish. They must obtain adequate oxygen and food, dispose of unwanted waste products, reproduce themselves, and monitor their environment and respond to changes. Single-celled animals like *Amoeba* do most of these things very simply, but have to lead simple lives.

Cells and More Cells

The next step in evolution was to have animals with many cells, arranged in two layers, an outer ectoderm and an inner endoderm. Sea anemones are arranged this way, tubes of cells, endoderm inwards, forming a sack-shaped gut for digesting food. Next, and a major step, was the development of a third cell layer, mesoderm, between the other two, from which organs such as muscles, and reproductive and excretory systems, can be made.

Having muscles organized by nerves encouraged the development of a head, the location for a primitive brain and sensors such as eye-spots. Flatworms are examples of this early evolutionary stage: their simple structure of a digestive tube, surrounded by muscles and other organs, contained in a roughly tubular skin of ectoderm, is the pattern followed by all other animals, although in most cases the forces of evolution have reshaped the basic design dramatically.

The next evolutionary step was the division of the body into segments. Earthworms are a primitive example, where, apart from the head, each segment contains a similar set of muscles, nerves and organs, and a section of gut. In arthropods such as insects and crabs, the limbs on each segment have evolved specialized structures and uses. Some are walking legs, some mouthparts, some perhaps wings or pinching claws. Here, instead of duplicate organs in each segment, a single heart has developed, pushing oxygen-carrying blood to working muscles and other organs in all parts of the body, and there is just one set of reproductive organs. Brains became larger, and senses of smell, taste and sight much better developed.

As multi-celled animals increased in size, so there became a need for body support. The arthropods developed an external skeleton (exoskeleton), which provided anchor points for stronger muscles for flight, and also provided body armour for defence against enemies and harsh environmental conditions. But an exoskeleton is also a box inside which the animal cannot grow, so it must be reabsorbed or shed at intervals and replaced with a larger one.

Vertebrates Arrive

The next major evolutionary step was the appearance of fish. Fish, amphibians, reptiles, birds, and mammals share the same basic skeletal layout, centred on a segmented, flexible backbone running from head to

Left: Inside the shell, or carapace, of the Galapagos giant tortoise is a skeleton of much the same pattern as a human's or dog's.

Right: The digestive systems of many animals share a common pattern: a mouth, passing into a gullet, then a stomach where digestion occurs; then sections of intestine where foods are absorbed.

VOLES BREED WHEN 15 DAYS OLD, HAVE TOTAL OF 150 YOUNG IN LIFETIME

tail. At the head end, skulls developed to protect the vital nerve and sense co-ordination centre, the brain. Along part of the backbone, ribs developed to protect vital organs and assist in breathing, particularly for animals abandoning aquatic life and living on land, which developed lungs for oxygen exchange. For movement, offshoot bones linked to the backbone became fin supports in fish. These developed into the clumsy limbs of amphibians and reptiles as these struggled to conquer the problems of life on dry land, and later evolved into the sophisticated wings of birds, and the huge, specialized range of mammal limbs. To lead such energetic lives, birds and mammals developed, separately, high-efficiency four-chambered hearts to pump blood to lungs and muscles, and evolved a body temperature-control mechanism, becoming warm-blooded and independent of environmental temperatures.

Beneath the wings of birds, the skin of lizards, the blubber of seals' flippers, and the hair of horses, are limb skeletons of the same basic design. Though this design may be modified tremendously by evolution and adaptation to suit the animals' way of life, all are based on the five-digit limbs just as in our own bodies.

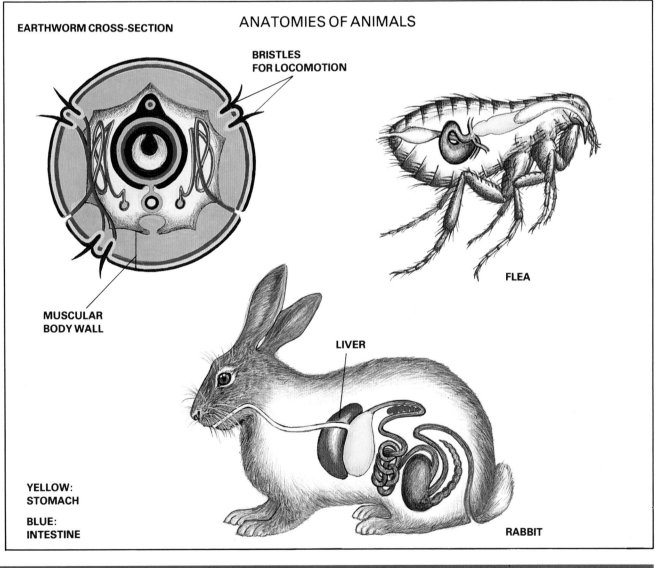

ANATOMIES OF ANIMALS

EARTHWORM CROSS-SECTION

BRISTLES FOR LOCOMOTION

MUSCULAR BODY WALL

FLEA

LIVER

YELLOW: STOMACH

BLUE: INTESTINE

RABBIT

HUMMINGBIRD WINGS BEAT 90 TIMES A SECOND • BARN OWL EATS 1,000 MICE IN YEAR

THE LIVES OF PLANTS

Plants are divided into two groups, flowerless "lower" plants, and "higher" plants which flower and set seeds. Plant life on earth is thought to have started from an ancestral microscopic alga, probably similar to *Euglena* that flourishes in ponds today. *Euglena* has one cell, with a nucleus containing its genetic database and with chlorophyll for photosynthesis. Such algae, and also bacteria, have the simplest form of reproduction in the plant kingdom. The cell contents condense, the nucleus divides, and two separate but identical new algae form and swim away.

Asexual Reproduction

In mosses, two distinct "alternating generations" occur. Conspicuous fruiting bodies, like swans' necks, shed spores which germinate to form branched filaments called protonemas. On protonemas, buds develop and grow into typical tufts of moss. These may be male or female, and carry their inconspicuous male or female sexual organs at their shoot tips. When ripe, male sperm from this sexual generation swim off to find and fertilize a mature female ovum, often on a different plant. This cross-fertilization allows genetic material from two different parent plants to mix. This also explains why mosses need damp habitats to flourish. Cells in the fertilized egg divide, producing a large embryo. This develops into a moss plant, put-ting up a swan's-neck stalk topped by a capsule which produces spores by simple cell division – asexual reproduction – to restart the cycle.

Sexual Reproduction

Seed-bearing plants have lost swimming sperms and the conspicuous alternation of generations, and are divided into two groups, gymnosperms and angiosperms. Gymnosperms have unisexual flowers lacking petals and sepals. Small male cones on coniferous trees, such as spruce, shed winged pollen grains that are blown to large receptive female cones, often on a tree some distance away. Between the scales of the female cones lie the eggs. Once the male pollen grain has landed, it may take a year to fuse fully and fertilize the female ovum, which in turn may take two more years to ripen before falling to the ground to germinate into a new miniature spruce tree.

Angiosperms usually have separate petals and sepals to their flowers, which are often elaborate and beautiful. Many can reproduce sexually and asexually, but the mixing of genetic material that takes place in sexual reproduction – in this case, pollination from another plant – is of great evolutionary value. Some bisexual plants have male and female organs in the same flower, others (monoecious) in different flowers but on the same plant. In these cases, the two sexes mature at different times to prevent self-pollination. In a typical flower, pollen is produced in anthers carried on stalks called stamens. Female ovules are

Left: Fungi, such as these fly agarics, lack chlorophyll, and thus cannot make their own food.

Right: Many plants employ clever methods to ensure they are pollinated. The bulbous lip of the bee orchid flower looks so like a bumble-bee that it fools other bees into attempting to mate with it. In the process, the yellow packets of pollen (pollinia) stick to the real bee's back and are carried off to fertilize another orchid.

PLANTS PROVIDE IMPORTANT MEDICINES, INCLUDING PENICILLIN AND ASPIRIN

carried in an ovary, on top of which the stigma projects to collect pollen grains.

Pollination Is a Must

Flower structure often indicates the means of pollination. Wind-pollinated plants, such as trees, have free-hanging male catkins ideal for shedding pollen into the breeze, and simple open stigmas to maximize their chances of trapping the pollen. Insect pollination offers better chances of successful fertilization, but first the insect must be attracted to the plant. The enormous diversity of curiously shaped flowers of a profusion of colours that characterizes many higher plants reflects this essential need to be pollinated. Sometimes scent and a supply of sugar-rich nectar add to the attraction. Flowers may be shaped to exclude all but the correct pollinator. Vetches (or peas) have keeled flowers that can be entered only by weighty and powerful bees.

LICHENS

Lichens are unusual but very effective co-operations of plants, composed of single-celled algae enmeshed in a fungus. Although they grow very slowly, they can survive in seemingly harsh conditions in all sorts of locations. Lichens provide food for animals, and humans have derived many medical benefits from them. They are also sensitive to pollution, particularly sulphur dioxide, a waste product from burning coal. A variety of forms is shown here.

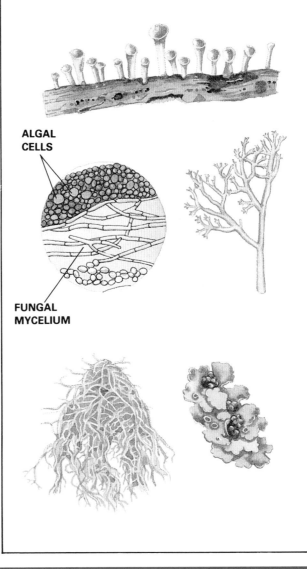

ALGAL CELLS

FUNGAL MYCELIUM

ALGAE GROW EVEN ON THE ANTARCTIC ICE CAP • LICHENS LIVE OVER 4,000 YEARS

HOW PLANTS GROW

Typical plants are composed of flowers, which later turn to seeds, plus stems and leaves, and a root. Roots serve various functions: through fine root hairs they extract from the soil water and minerals essential for plant growth, and anchor the whole plant firmly to the ground. In some plants, such as carrots and turnips, they also serve as a food store. Some plants growing in exposed habitats hug the ground and have very reduced stems, but most, including trees, need their leaves exposed to air and sunlight for efficient photosynthesis. For these to avoid shading from competitive plants nearby, strong stems and branches are vital to ensure the best position for leaves and flowers.

Living and Surviving

Green leaves are plants' food-producing organs. They occur in a multitude of shapes, formed by evolution to

Below: Bromeliads are epiphytes, plants which grow on other plants, usually without feeding on them. Some roots hold them to the branch. Others hang free and absorb moisture from the jungle air.

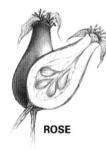

ROSE

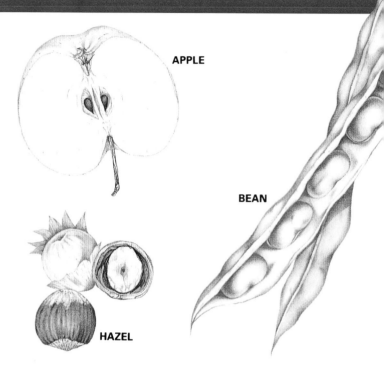

APPLE

BEAN

HAZEL

suit particular life styles and habitats. Needle-like leaves of conifers can withstand drought on sandy soils, and winter snow, while the shiny leaves of jungle plants, where rainfall is often excessive, have a pointed tip to encourage water to run off quickly.

The fundamental unit of plant anatomy is the cell. Boxed in by a rigid cellulose wall, it contains a jelly-like cytoplasm in which are the nucleus (containing genetic information coded onto chromosomes) and several mitochondria (which control cell energy production). In cells of green parts of the plant are chloroplasts, containing the pigment chlorophyll, which is responsible for harnessing the sun's energy to manufacture carbohydrates. These major plant foods are usually made in the leaves, where a waterproof cuticle, or skin, prevents water loss.

Large plants need reinforcement to hold them upright, usually found as strong fibres or as woody thickening to cell walls. Vascular cells are the "plumbing", essential to transport food and water around the plant. Xylem vessels carry water, while phloem carries food manufactured in the leaves. These vessels occur in bundles like veins, grouped with reinforcing fibres. Areas called cambium are responsible for cell multi-

TALLEST TREE KNOWN – AUSTRALIAN EUCALYPTUS OVER 150 m MEASURED IN 1872

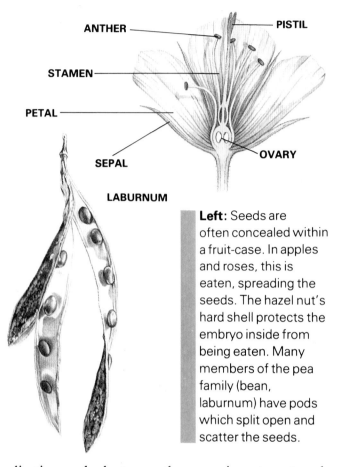

ANTHER — PISTIL
STAMEN —
PETAL —
SEPAL
OVARY
LABURNUM

Left: Seeds are often concealed within a fruit-case. In apples and roses, this is eaten, spreading the seeds. The hazel nut's hard shell protects the embryo inside from being eaten. Many members of the pea family (bean, laburnum) have pods which split open and scatter the seeds.

which allow plants to spread without seeding, is one. Asexual reproduction, common among lower plants (p. 14), provides a simple way of increasing numbers, but in neither vegetative nor asexual reproduction is there any mixing of genetic material – the offspring are all identical, clones of their parent. If all goes well, this is a simple and effective method, until conditions change, when the flexibility needed for adaptation and evolution is lacking. For this reason, most plants also have some form of sexual reproduction, because, when cross-fertilization occurs, there is a mixing of genetic material from a wider gene pool and this gives that flexibility, which could be invaluable.

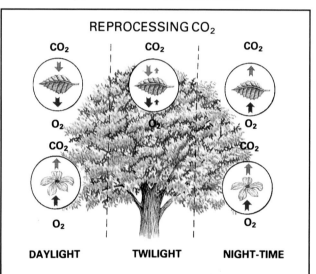

REPROCESSING CO_2

CO_2 CO_2 CO_2

O_2 O_2 O_2

CO_2 CO_2

O_2 O_2

DAYLIGHT **TWILIGHT** **NIGHT-TIME**

During the daytime under the influence of sunlight and with chlorophyll as the catalyst, trees and other green plants manufacture their food through the process of photosynthesis. Carbon dioxide (CO_2) is used, and oxygen (O_2) released. At the same time, the plant is breathing, using O_2 and releasing CO_2. As photosynthesis is quicker at this time, the overall effect is for the significant O_2 release to enrich the atmosphere, allowing animals the vital resource they need to breathe and survive. In periods of low sunlight, such as twilight, breathing continues, while photosynthesis slows down. During night-time, there is no photosynthesis, so overall the tree is absorbing some O_2 and releasing some CO_2.

plication and plant growth, occurring at root and shoot tips and also around stems to cope with increasing girth. In stems or trunks, they add pith cells internally and layers of corky protective bark externally.

Outside tropical regions, surviving the winter is a major problem for many plants. Some reduce their above-ground leaves to a weatherproof minimum: deciduous trees shed their leaves, while thistles and many other plants lose stems and leaves and rely on food stored in roots or stolons protected from climatic extremes below ground. From these, fresh plants will sprout next spring. These are perennials, living for several years. Annual plants have evolved different tactics: each year they die, leaving only seeds protected in robust coats, ready to germinate the next year.

Cloning and Gene-mixing

Plants have three main ways of reproducing themselves and increasing their numbers. Vegetative reproduction, the production of runners or bulbils

LIFE IN THE SEA

Salt water covers almost 70 per cent of the earth's surface, making this by far the largest of all habitats. There are four major oceans, Atlantic, Arctic, Indian and Pacific, of which the Pacific is the largest (over 160 million sq km) and the Arctic the smallest (14 million sq km).

Seas rich in plankton form a monster soup, composed of minute algae and countless millions of shrimps and tiny larval stages of various shellfish, crabs, worms, sea urchins, and the like. Plankton is the basic food of huge numbers of fish and birds (and amazingly some whales), while on these other fish and

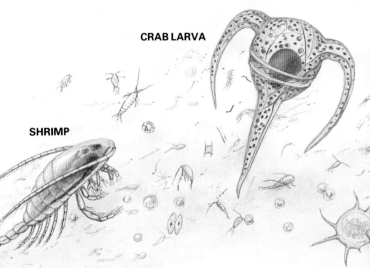

CRAB LARVA

SHRIMP

FISH EGG

WORM LARVA

Above: Billions of minute plants and animals form the plankton of the sea.

birds flourish as predators or pirates. Seaweeds are abundant algae in which the green chlorophyll is sometimes masked by red or brown pigments. They flourish near the coast and in water less than 100 m deep because they need light for photosynthesis.

Remarkable Variety

Fish occur in a truly phenomenal range of colours, sizes and shapes, and their various anatomical adaptations to marine life are just as remarkable. Flatfish such as sole are able to mimic the colours of the seabed. Some seahorses have oddly lobed fins which closely resemble the seaweed fronds among which they live. Male seahorses have pouches on their bellies in which females place their eggs, and where the young seahorses rush back to safety if danger threatens. But, basically, there are two kinds of fish: elasmobranchs which have gristly cartilaginous skeletons, and teleosts with bony skeletons.

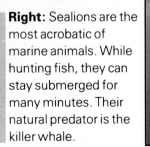

Right: Sealions are the most acrobatic of marine animals. While hunting fish, they can stay submerged for many minutes. Their natural predator is the killer whale.

GANNETS NESTING ON ST KILDA CATCH 120 TONNES OF FISH EVERY DAY

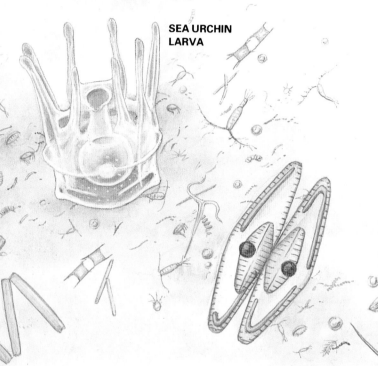

SEA URCHIN LARVA

at which they are submerged, so bony fish can adjust their swimming level in the sea.

Many Predators

Few sea fish are vegetarians, most living on plankton or fish smaller than themselves. Living on these, in turn, are predatory seals, whales and porpoises, and many fish-eating birds. Some, such as skuas and frigatebirds, are pirates, chasing other seabirds in flight and harassing them into coughing up their catch, which the pirate often catches and gobbles down before it reaches the sea. Others, such as gannets, fish for themselves by diving headlong into the water, often from 20 m. Gannets have tough feathers and thick skins lined with an elastic layer of fat, and their eyes are set in padded sockets, all to absorb the impact of hitting the sea at speed.

CILIA KEEP PLANKTON AFLOAT

Best known of elasmobranchs are dogfish, rays and sharks. Great white sharks are the super-predators, but not all members of the group are ferocious hunters. Largest of all fish is the whale shark, a placid 14-m monster feeding on microscopic plankton and krill that it filters from giant mouthfuls of seawater. Skates and rays are flattened, many living on the sea-bed and excellently camouflaged. Some deliver powerful electric shocks to stun their prey, others defend themselves with a poisoned dagger set in their tail. Most spectacular is the devilfish, or manta ray, of the open oceans. It has a "wingspan" of up to 7 m, and weighs as much as 1,400 kg. Like the whale shark, it feeds on plankton and shrimps.

Sharks must keep swimming or they sink to the sea-bed, because they are slightly denser than water. Bony fish (teleosts) such as herring do not have this problem since they have swimbladders in their bodies. The amount of oxygen in the bladders can be controlled by extracting more from the herring's blood, or allowing the blood to reabsorb it. This changes the herring's buoyancy: the more gas in its swimbladder, the lower its density. Just as submarines pump compressed air in or out of their buoyancy tanks to control the depth

Below: Unique among lizards, the marine iguana dives into surf to feed on seaweed.

THE OPEN OCEAN

The ocean floor is not flat. Beneath the sea are mountain ridges with peaks rising to 2,000 m, some of them active volcanoes. Between them are valleys, called trenches, the deepest (off Guam in the Pacific) plunging to 11,000 m below sea level. Everywhere is a layer of ooze many metres thick, composed of sand and silt washed out by the world's major rivers, mixed with sedimentary remains of countless millions of ocean creatures large and small.

Below 100 m, not enough daylight penetrates for seaweeds to grow, and below 300 m the ocean is permanently dark, usually cold (about 4 °C) and comparatively still compared with surface waves. Despite the cold and darkness, there is still plenty of life. The deepest-living residents have only recently been discovered: pale blind crabs, giant clams and 3-m-long worms, at 3,000 m below the surface, getting their food from hot mineral-rich water coming from a volcanic crack off the Pacific coast of South America.

Danger in the Dark

Specialist fish can live in total darkness down to 3,000 m. Some have huge eyes, while others carry their own phosphorescent lighting systems with them, to keep contact with others and to attract mates. Angler fish in shallow seas live on the seabed, with a spine like a fishing rod over their heads, dangling a shrimp-like piece of skin at the end. This bait lures inquisitive fish within reach of the huge angler fish jaws, which open like a trap to grab their prey. Deep-ocean angler fish use similar tactics, but their "bait" is illuminated. Colonies of bacteria live within the fish's lure and produce a greenish glow.

Huge Ocean Mammals

Seals and whales are the only mammals to master the ocean depths. Sperm whales can stay submerged at depths of over 2,000 m for up to two hours, hunting giant squid, their favourite prey. Giant squid can reach 30 m long and put up a good fight; squid sucker marks the size of dinner plates have been found on whales' skin. Sperm whales are "toothed" whales, with huge heads taking up one-third of their length, and with jaws armed with a fearsome array of teeth.

Nearer the ocean surface, the other type of whale, "baleen" or "whalebone", hunt completely different food. Blue whales, 33 m long and weighing up to 130 tonnes, are the largest animals ever to have lived on earth, their size being possible only because of the supporting buoyancy given by the water. Unbelievably, these ocean giants feed mostly on shrimps called krill. Their huge mouths are edged with sheets of whalebone, like enormous brooms. They gulp a gigantic mouthful, then force water out through the whalebone, filtering out their meal of krill. Whales are the only truly marine mammals spending all their lives in the sea – including mating and giving birth, which seals do on land. Whales still must breathe air, and surface regularly to do this, emptying their lungs through the nostril on top of their head to give the distinctive spout of water and water vapour.

Master Gliders

Albatrosses hunt over Southern Hemisphere oceans. Unlike whales, they come to land to breed, but even when feeding their nestling they may hunt fish thousands of kilometres from home. With long slender wings spanning 3 m, albatrosses are master gliders.

Right: All the creatures of the ocean, from the enormous sperm whale to the small brittlestar, must be able to move and hunt for food in the cold, darkness and tremendous pressures of the ocean depths.

DEEP-SEA JELLYFISH

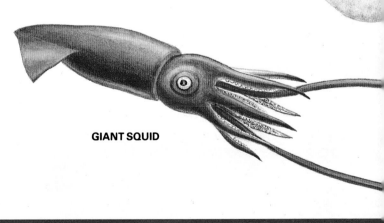

GIANT SQUID

Most live in windy latitudes below 40 °S. Permanently windy conditions are ideal for albatrosses, because their technique is to glide across the wind, slowly losing height, before turning sharply into the wind, which lifts them steeply for 30 or 40 m; having climbed without a wingbeat, they turn and glide off again, covering hundreds of kilometres daily.

CUTTLEFISH

ANGLER FISH

PELICAN EEL

BRITTLESTAR

SPERM WHALE

GIANT OCTOPUS

DEEP-SEA SWIMMING SEA CUCUMBER

ATLANTIC GIANT SQUID REACH   17 m LONG

ON THE BEACH

Long sandy beaches may be ideal for human summer holidays, but they are among the most difficult of all habitats for wildlife. Survival is a struggle, as the millions of grains of sand or pebbles are always on the move, either blown by the wind into shifting sand dunes on the beach or swept around by the waves below high-water mark. This makes establishing a firm base equally difficult for animals and plants.

For plants, conditions on the beach are made more difficult by the drying effect of salty winds, and strong winds are more frequent on the coast than inland. Some find shelter in valleys between the sand hills, where rainwater gathers in pools called dune slacks. Strong winds may shift the dunes themselves, the blown sand smothering the dune slack and its wildlife, so this is a hazardous existence. On dunes themselves, marram grass is one of the few plants able to survive, and it is often planted along coasts to hold the sand dunes in place. Marram grass leaves have a tough silica coating, and are rolled inwards to protect the stomata from the wind and reduce water loss.

Beneath Your Feet

The most successful beach animals are the molluscs, or shellfish. Usually all that can be seen are the shells of long-dead animals, but once the incoming tide has covered the sand the beach comes to life. Buried several centimetres in the sand, the bivalve shellfish push up fleshy tubes like drinking straws. They suck passing water down the tube, sift out food particles, and pump it out again. They can move about, using a powerful muscular foot to drag them through the sand. If caught unawares by a falling tide, razor shells 10 cm long can bury themselves in seconds to escape from marauding gulls. There are also many brightly coloured worms in the sand, living in burrows whose walls are linked with hardened saliva to prevent them caving in.

Not only gulls hunt here, but also starfish. On the underside of their arms, starfish have hundreds of tiny suckers called tube feet. These are worked by hydraulic pressure, allowing starfish to move slowly about, and to prize open the tightest-shut clam. The starfish then pushes its stomach inside out through its mouth, wrapping it around its prey before swallowing it.

Seabed Specialists

Just offshore live flatfish such as plaice. When they hatch, young plaice look just like other fish, with an

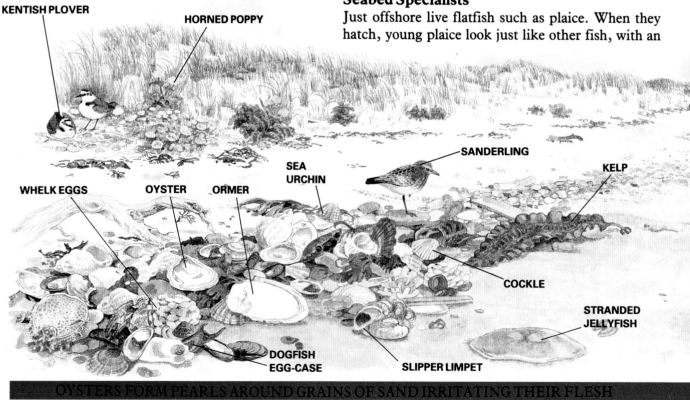

KENTISH PLOVER

HORNED POPPY

SANDERLING

KELP

SEA URCHIN

WHELK EGGS

OYSTER

ORMER

COCKLE

STRANDED JELLYFISH

DOGFISH EGG-CASE

SLIPPER LIMPET

OYSTERS FORM PEARLS AROUND GRAINS OF SAND IRRITATING THEIR FLESH

upright dorsal fin and tail, and an eye on each side of their head. Soon they sink to the sandy floor, and lie on one side – in some species the left, in others the right. The eye underneath slowly moves around the head until it, too, is on top, and the mouth also moves around on top so that with each bite plaice do not get a mouthful of sand. The skin of the underside becomes white, while the upper surface quickly takes on the speckled colours of the sand. Flat on the seabed, the plaice is almost impossible to spot, and, if it moves, special skin cells allow it to change colour quickly to match its new background.

Above the Tideline

For birds that nest on the beach, good camouflage is essential. Sandy-coloured Kentish or snowy plovers scrape shallow saucer nests and lay four speckled eggs perfectly camouflaged against the sand. Chicks, too, are excellently camouflaged. If they are running about feeding when their parent sounds the alarm, the chicks crouch immediately. White necks which showed up well to let the parents know their whereabouts become invisible instantly. They stay crouched no matter how close danger comes, because their lives may depend on the efficiency of their camouflage. Being trodden on by an unwary human is then the main threat to eggs and chicks.

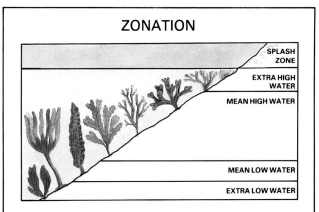

ZONATION

SPLASH ZONE

EXTRA HIGH WATER

MEAN HIGH WATER

MEAN LOW WATER

EXTRA LOW WATER

Marine algae, better known as seaweeds, occur in distinct zones on the shore. Each species is best adapted to a particular set of conditions, reflecting its ability to tolerate exposure to air and immersion in water. This is often related to the positions of the tides. In this way, competition between species for space and food resources is reduced to a minimum.

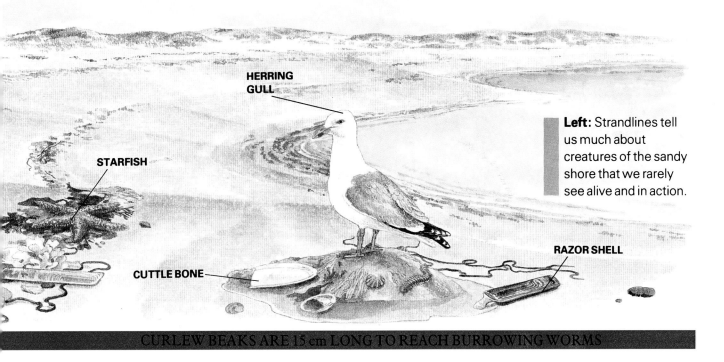

HERRING GULL

STARFISH

CUTTLE BONE

RAZOR SHELL

Left: Strandlines tell us much about creatures of the sandy shore that we rarely see alive and in action.

CURLEW BEAKS ARE 15 cm LONG TO REACH BURROWING WORMS

LIFE ON THE CLIFFS

TUFTED PUFFIN

RHINOCEROS AUKLET

KITTIWAKE

GUILLEMOT

BLACK GUILLEMOT

ANCIENT MURRELET

PELAGIC CORMORANT

WESTERN GULL

BLACK OYSTERCATCHER

BLACK TURNSTONE

BRANDT'S CORMORANT

In many parts of the world, land meets sea in towering rocky cliffs. Pounding waves have created a vertical habitat, where exposure to fierce seas and wind, and continuous drenching in salt water make life difficult for plants and animals.

Finding a Foothold

For plants, just securing a roothold on the rock face is hazardous enough. Roots must penetrate deep into cracks in search of fresh water, and leaves are usually fleshy, containing cells to store scarce water. They are often waxy, or grey with downy hairs, with few stomata. This helps cut down water loss through the leaves. This is the home of specialist plants such as thrift, scurvygrass and samphire.

At the base of the cliff where the waves break, life is even more hazardous. The only plants to survive are lichens, strange but successful cooperative plants where single-celled algae grow embedded in fungus. Those growing nearest the water are blackish, and so well attached to the rocks that they look like a coat of paint. Higher up, greenish lichens appear, and at the top of the cliff are the striking orange discs of *Xanthoria*, like miniature pie crusts.

Animals making a home year-round at the foot of the cliff have to be equally robust. Specialist shellfish can survive, and do so in masses, because living clustered together gives them extra protection from the seas. Conical limpets hold tight with a powerful sucker foot, but wander off beneath the water at high tide to rasp lichens off the rocks with their file-like tongue. They always return to the same spot on the rocks, because here their shell is shaped to fit tight.

Also present in huge numbers are white-shelled barnacles. Although they look like molluscs, they are actually crustaceans, small shrimps protected by

SEABIRDS ARE STILL EATEN BY HUMANS ON REMOTE ISLANDS

plates of shell. These plates open when the tide is in, and inside is a shrimp, lying on its back and kicking food into its mouth with feathery feet that stick out through the gap in the shell.

Life in Pools

Rock pools are more sheltered. Small seaweeds live here, and many differently coloured anemones have their fringes of tentacles waving in the currents. Anemones are not plants, but animals called coelenterates, related to jellyfish. They catch their tiny animal food by harpooning it with microscopic darts fired from the tentacles when they are touched. The tentacles wrap around prey and convey it to the central mouth. In these pools small fish such as blennies, with fins shaped like legs, can walk about on the rocks. Here, too, live whelks, spiral-shelled sea snails. Whelks are predatory molluscs, using acid saliva and rough tongues to drill through shells of other molluscs to eat the animal inside.

On the Rocks

Turnstones are typical shore birds, feeding at the water's edge, excellently camouflaged against the seaweed. They use their shovel-shaped beaks to turn over stones and seaweed to find the small creatures hiding beneath. Larger and brighter, the pied oystercatcher is even more noticeable through its shrill piping calls.

On the cliffs, ledges are put to good use in summer by colonies of nesting seabirds. Predators such as rats and foxes cannot reach these ledges, so their eggs and young are safe. Many gulls nest here, including ocean-going kittiwakes, which can glue their muddy nest even under the arched roof of a cave. They must have the best-behaved young of all birds, because more than one step away from the nest before they can fly must mean certain death.

Left: In suitable areas, every space on a rocky shore will be occupied by breeding seabirds during the spring and early summer. This cliff shows some Northeast Pacific species.

Right: Cliff plants survive in scarce soil in the smallest cracks, and withstand wind and salt spray. Scurvygrass (top), basil thyme (centre) and yellow whitlowgrass (bottom) are shown.

TALLEST CLIFF 1,005 m, IN HAWAII · LAST GREAT AUK WAS KILLED IN 1842

LIFE IN RIVERS

Rivers and streams vary greatly. In hill country they run fast and clear over a gravel bed, but in the lowlands their flow is much slower and the water muddy with fine soil particles washed from the land.

Inland Waters

Plenty of oxygen dissolves in clear upland streams as they sparkle over rocky shallows. Waterweeds are plentiful, firmly anchored to large rocks and totally submerged. They are rich in shrimps and caddis flies, food for fish such as trout living in deeper pools. Specialist birds of these rivers are dippers. Thrush-sized but wren-like in build, they bob incessantly while perching on mid-stream boulders. Suddenly they walk straight into the rushing waters, quickly submerging. In the shallows, they hunt caddis flies and water scorpions on foot, clinging to the stream bed with powerful claws. In deeper water they use their wings to swim, bobbing out jauntily many metres away, white belly prominent.

Oxygen levels are lower in slow, silty rivers, and much less plant growth survives in the turbid waters. On quieter stretches, bulrushes or papyrus will flourish along the banks. Elephant fish are specially adapted to live in murky African rivers. They find their way about, and communicate with each other, by giving off regular electric pulses, which bounce off objects in their path. Should they swim into polluted water, elephant fish produce a quick-fire stream of discharge clicks, which alert other elephant fish to the dangers ahead. Because they are so sensitive to even low levels of pollution, water engineers now use elephant fish, in an aquarium, to test water quality, displaying their patterns of electrical discharges on television monitors.

Towards the Sea

Estuaries form where rivers, broad, muddy and sluggish now, meet the sea. Here mineral richness washed out of the land mingles with the goodness carried in by the sea, the whole rich system recharged twice daily by the comings and goings of the tide. Mudflats may look sterile and inhospitable, but they are far more sheltered than coastal beaches. Often foul-smelling, this muddy ooze absolutely teems with small animals.

Among the plants, single-celled algae predominate, but some specialists can survive the frequent changes in salinity and the regular drying-out at low tide. *Zostera*, an unusual marine grass, is one of them, favourite food for wigeon and brent geese. Stiff tufts of rice grass poke up through the mud, and silt gathers around the base of these clumps, raising the mud level until eventually a new island is formed. On estuary islands, salt-tolerant grasses grow along with specialist plants such as sea aster and sea lavender.

Although estuaries may provide a summer home to some breeding ducks, waders and gulls, it is in au-

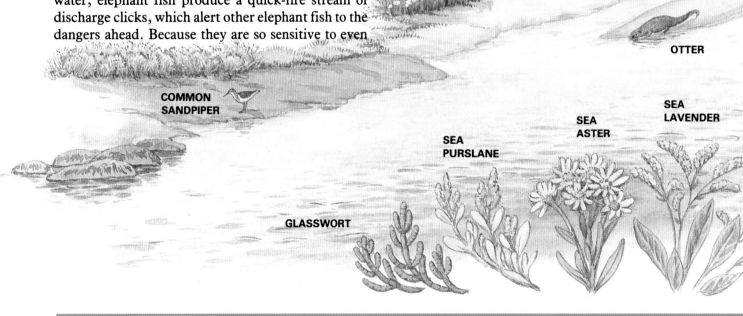

OTTER

COMMON SANDPIPER

SEA LAVENDER

SEA ASTER

SEA PURSLANE

GLASSWORT

PIRANHA FISH REPORTEDLY ATE TROOP OF MEXICAN CAVALRY FORDING A RIVER

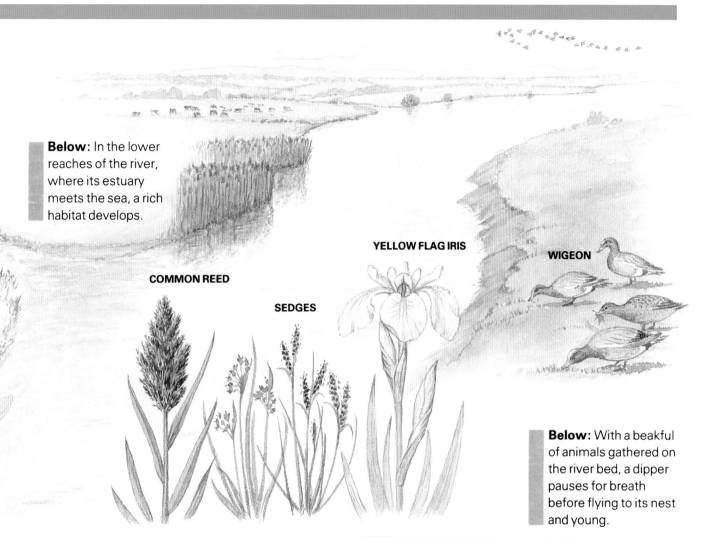

Below: In the lower reaches of the river, where its estuary meets the sea, a rich habitat develops.

YELLOW FLAG IRIS

COMMON REED

SEDGES

WIGEON

Below: With a beakful of animals gathered on the river bed, a dipper pauses for breath before flying to its nest and young.

tumn, winter and spring that their phenomenal richness is of most value to the wildlife community. The ooze is home to countless small worms, shellfish and crustaceans, often totalling millions to each square metre. These are the food supply of vast flocks of ducks, geese and particularly wading birds.

Some waders and wildfowl spend the whole winter on one estuary, while others use them as staging posts on their long migratory journeys. They will be regular visitors each year, arriving in spring and feeding non-stop on the estuary animals, recharging their food and energy reserves, refuelling for the next long haul of the journey to their breeding grounds. In autumn, the reverse journey is less hurried, with many waders pausing for some weeks to change their feathers, moulting in the sheltered safety of an estuary.

ELECTRIC EELS CAN PRODUCE ENOUGH ELECTRICITY TO KILL A COW

POND AND LAKE LIFE

In the still waters of ponds and lakes, the silt that clouded the water of lowland rivers can settle, allowing the water to clear and a rich plant life to develop. Some plants such as water lilies root in the nutrient-rich silt on the bottom, sending up floating leaves and flowers to the surface. Others float free, smaller plants such as duckweed relying on the surface tension to keep them afloat. Larger plants such as water hyacinth have buoyancy tanks of air-filled cells built into their stems.

Huge numbers of animals live among the waterweed, for this is the richest freshwater habitat. Under a microscope, a drop of pond water teems with life. Single-celled *Amoeba* and *Paramecium* abound, as do bouncy water fleas, which, though larger, are best seen magnified. This mass of small animals is called freshwater plankton, and is the food supply for larger animals ranging from tadpoles to fish. On small fish, larger predatory fish such as the ferocious pike, weighing several kilos, feed.

On the Surface

Pond skaters use surface tension to support their tiny weight, only their large and bristly feet in contact with the water. They dash about in search of insects less fortunate than themselves floundering in the water. Skaters attack, extracting the body juices of their prey with long sucking mouthparts. Just below the surface, water boatmen swim upside down, their greater weight buoyed up in the water. One pair of legs is modified and looks like oars, which the boatmen use to row about in search of prey. They have shorter, stabbing mouthparts and tackle bigger prey than skaters, even biting human fingers! Water boatmen can fly to a fresh pond if theirs dries up, using wings normally folded away out of sight.

Aerial Hunters

Flying over the water are dragonflies, their bulbous eyes giving the appearance of a helicopter as they hover and dart about in all directions on shimmering wings. Adult dragonflies have eyes excellent at detecting the slightest movement, and catch fast-moving flies in mid-air. Dragonfly larvae are wingless, and spend up to four years lurking underwater in the waterweed. Ferocious predators with huge jaws, they attack tadpoles and small fish. They grow steadily,

Right: A water spider gathers air on its body, carrying it down to fill its diving-bell nest in the pond weed.

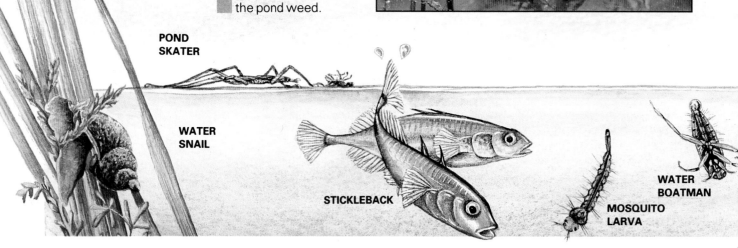

POND SKATER

WATER SNAIL

STICKLEBACK

MOSQUITO LARVA

WATER BOATMAN

GOLIATH FROG FROM AFRICA WEIGHS 3.3 kg • BULLFROG JUMPS 6.5 m

Left: The African jacana lives up to its other name, lily-trotter. It uses long toes to spread its weight on floating leaves.

Below: Beneath the still surface of a pond, snails graze on the weedier plants, while a wide range of predators hunt beneath and over the water.

eventually crawling up a reed stem to emerge into the air. Slowly the skin splits, and out crawls the adult dragonfly. As it dries, its crumpled new wings are pumped up by blood pressure in the veins to expand and harden. Once free-flying, adults often move away from water, taking up territory in a woodland glade, returning a year or more later to establish a territory over the lake, find a mate and breed.

Bird Predators

Predatory birds gather to exploit this wealth of lake life. Little grebes spend most of their lives on lakes. Hunting small fish, they dive leaving hardly a ripple, and can stay under for about a minute. Grebe feet have long toes with lobes of skin along the sides, and are positioned back near the tail to give maximum underwater propulsion.

Overhanging branches provide hunting perches for kingfishers. Waiting silently, kingfishers have to adjust their aim to allow for the way water distorts light rays. This makes ponds look shallower than they actually are, and target fish seem nearer the surface. Long experience gives kingfishers the necessary skills, and they dive, submerging to grab their fish. Back on the perch, prey is stunned by banging its head on the branch, before being swallowed head-first so that the spiny fins do not stick in the kingfisher's throat. Kingfishers nest in burrows excavated in lakeside banks. As the chicks grow, these burrows get smelly and slimy with old fish remains. When they fly out, parent kingfishers immediately dunk themselves in the water to clean up.

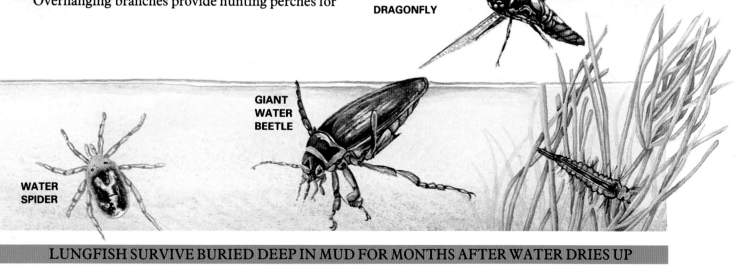

DRAGONFLY

GIANT WATER BEETLE

WATER SPIDER

LUNGFISH SURVIVE BURIED DEEP IN MUD FOR MONTHS AFTER WATER DRIES UP

MARSHES AND SWAMPS

Swamps are a very specialized habitat, liable to sudden floods. They are dangerous for heavy animals, which can sink into the boggy ground which quakes like jelly at every step, and difficult for lightweight ones because of the lush tangled vegetation. But this does not prevent heavy animals like elephant and water buffalo seeking to relax in the mud. These tropical animals feel the heat, and because of their size have difficulty finding enough shade. Wallowing in the mud cools them, and when they emerge the caked mud dries on their skins. This helps protect even their

Above right: A male sitatunga ventures out into the open, a rare event for this African reedbed antelope.

Above: This Asian wetland is one of the natural world's richest ecological resources.

thick skins from sunburn, and, more important, forms a layer through which mosquitoes or tsetse flies cannot bite to suck blood, so it works as a very effective defence against annoying insects.

Dangerous Traps

Swamps have always been dangerous, even for the largest animals, and many of the best fossils of creatures living millions of years ago were formed from animals that died trapped in swamps and later turned into rock. One of the few living animals specially adapted to swamp conditions is the sitatunga, an African antelope the size of a large dog. Sitatunga have split hooves like other antelopes, but they are long and flexibly jointed. In deep water, sitatunga walk on tiptoe – on platform soles – while, when hurrying across soft mud, the hooves splay out to provide extra support to stop them sinking.

Spreading the Load

Long toes also help stop members of the heron family from sinking when they hunt frogs, fish and eels in

EUROPEAN CATFISH OR WELS REACH 4.5 m – ARE REPORTED TO HAVE EATEN CHILDREN

swamps. Herons hunt stealthily, taking slow paces to avoid disturbing prey. Their eyes can swivel in their sockets to look vertically downwards, even if the beak is pointing to the sky. No movement betrays them, until a sudden stab from the dagger-shaped beak secures the prey. Only when it strikes is the full length of the heron's snake-like neck revealed.

Bitterns belong to the heron family and live full-time in reedbeds. Secretive, they are rarely seen but often heard as they produce a foghorn-like booming call that earned them the name "bog bumper" in the

MASTERBUILDER MIGRANT

The power of flight and being able to perch in the vegetation allow other birds to live in treacherous swamps without danger, and to feed on the rich insect life that flourishes there. Reed warblers are summer visitors to European and Asian reedbeds, migrating from Africa. In spring, males migrate first, travelling overnight and feeding during the day. On arrival they set up territories, and in the early days of summer sing for most of the night. This is to attract down the females, also migrating at night high overhead.

Reed warbler nests are masterpieces of construction, woven from strands of reed leaves around a group of vertical stems. So effective are the basketwork handles that the warblers weave, using only their beaks and feet, that the nest does not slip down even when gales lash the reeds. Cuckoos often lay their egg in reed warbler nests, and the nest is strong enough even to take the weight of the young cuckoo, which dwarfs its foster parents.

Below: The goliath heron is the largest of the heron family. After a patient wait, standing quiet and motionless, this one has stabbed a 40-cm bass.

past. Bitterns have striped yellow, black and brown plumage, and if frightened stand bolt upright, beak pointing to the sky. So slim are they that their striped plumage gives them perfect camouflage to merge into their reed-stem background. Bitterns have special feathers producing a kind of powder, and on each foot one claw serrated like a comb. Both powder and comb are used to clean up the feathers after a meal of slimy eels, frogs or fish, because clean-cared-for plumage is essential if birds are to fly well and keep warm.

DOWN ON THE FARM

No habitat is more often disturbed than farmland. On arable farms, each year the entire habitat is destroyed for many plants and animals as the farmer harvests the crop and then ploughs the field. The birds can fly, the rabbits can run away, but for the plants and smaller animals there is little chance of escape, although some insects and other small animals will escape by burrowing deep, or as eggs or larvae, protected in a shell or case until favourable conditions return. Plants tend to be annuals, and survive as seeds in the soil until the next spring.

History of Farmland

As recently as 2,000 years ago, much of the landscape was covered in scrub or, more often, woodland or forest. Human populations were small, and people lived by hunting wild animals. Gradually they took to domesticating animals and keeping them in herds, and then to clearing patches of forest to grow the first primitive crops of food, ancestors of the high-yielding wheat, cabbages and potatoes that farmers grow today. As the tribes settled down, they increased in numbers. They needed more land to grow food, and started to make homes. First of all these were rough shelters made out of branches, but, by 600 years ago, large houses were being made from sawn-up trees, and some of these houses are still standing. It took about 700 oak trees to make the roof of a large building such as a castle or cathedral, and about the same number to build a galleon. Wood was also the main fuel. As a result, more and more fields began to appear and the forests vanished.

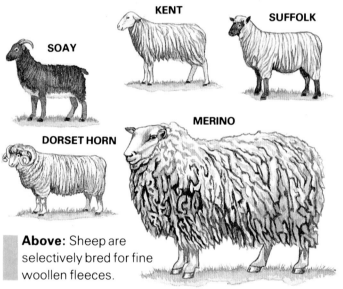

Above: Sheep are selectively bred for fine woollen fleeces.

Changes for the Better

These changes have created a farmland scenery where woods and copses are joined by the hedges which surround the fields. Woods act as wildlife reservoirs, and the hedges serve as the pipelines along which wildlife can move. After fields are harvested or cultivated, wildlife can move back in from these reservoirs as soon as a new crop starts to grow.

Where there are good hedges and plenty of woods and copses, the habitat that farmers have helped to create is actually much richer than the original forest it replaced. Deciduous forest in temperate climates is not a rich wildlife habitat, and most of the animals and plants that occur are found around the edges or in forest clearings. Farmland has a tremendous length of edge, and in consequence wildlife can flourish. Voles and mice and their main predators, weasels and stoats, do well; rabbits succeed rather too well, as they have taken a liking to crops and have become pests, but this has led to an increase in foxes. Many birds, too, have become more widespread in hedges and copses.

Modern Farming

In the last 50 years, farming has changed, sometimes not for the better. Bigger combine harvesters have encouraged bigger fields – made larger by pulling out the hedges. This destroys the network of pathways that wildlife can use to move around the countryside. Fortunately, these "prairie farms" are not proving to be successful, and are now not popular. Farmyard man-

Left: Adaptable birds, black-headed and common gulls have forsaken the shore to feed on worms turned up by the plough.

Left and right: Over thousands of years of domestication, mankind has tamed wild animals.

WILD BOAR

TAMWORTH

Left: Careful breeding has shaped pigs to give birth to larger litters of piglets ideal for meat production.

LARGE WHITE

ure has been replaced by man-made chemical fertilizers, leading to pollution of water supplies with nitrates harmful to health. Men and women with hoes have been replaced by weedkiller sprays that kill all plants except the crop, and may drift onto the headlands and kill the wildflowers.

Fortunately, again our attitudes are changing. No longer are the super-efficient pesticides chosen, because they often killed friend and foe alike in the crop, and there was always the risk that poisonous pollutants would reach us in our food. Now farmers use biological control as often as they can, using natural enemies such as predatory insects and even virus diseases to keep pests under control without harming the rest of the environment.

FINCH BEAKS

In the finch family, beaks vary according to their major foods. The long beak of the goldfinch can extract thistle seeds, while the rounded beak of the bullfinch helps it eat buds in winter. Hawfinches can crack open damson stones, while chaffinches tackle much smaller, softer-husked seeds. The extraordinary crossbill scissor-like beak can extract conifer seeds from their protective cone.

GOLDFINCH

BULLFINCH

HAWFINCH

CHAFFINCH

CROSSBILL

IN S AFRICA, 100 MILLION QUELEA KILLED AS AGRICULTURAL PESTS IN ONE YEAR

KESTREL

PIGEONS

ULLS ON REFUSE

FIREWEED

ELDER

INTRODUCED
PLANTS

GIANT
HOGWEED

CAT
CHASING
BIRDS

SMALL
TORTOISESHELL
BUTTERFLY

vide habitats where wildlife loses its fear of people. Even sites of building demolition attract wildlife. Fireweed (or rosebay willowherb) covers heaps of rubble with its pink blossom spikes, while later in the year buddleia, which establishes a roothold even between concrete slabs, flowers and attracts butterflies in profusion. Black redstarts, properly at home on mountainside rocky screes, find city rooftops and rubble just as good a habitat – even peregrine falcons, too, have nested on city blocks.

Above: Despite dangers like pollution, cats and traffic, urban areas with wasteland and gardens provide a rich habitat for plants and animals. Animals such as foxes are increasingly familiar urban visitors.

STARLINGS ROOST IN CITIES AS TEMPERATURES MAY BE 3 °C HIGHER THAN IN WOODS

HEATHLAND LIFE

GRASSHOPPER

BEE ORCHID

PRAYING MANTIS

Below: Ferocious spines guard the leaves of the acacia (top) and succulent euphorbia from grazing animals.

Within the term heathland fall several related habitats. All are open landscapes dotted with bushes or clumps of trees. Most are on soils comparatively low in nutrients, but this poor soil often passes unnoticed so attractive, colourful and specialized are the flowering plants that cover it.

Moorland

Most moors occur on high ground, often above 500 m, where soils are damp, peaty and acid, often with such poor drainage that bogs form. Mosses, particularly *Sphagnum*, are characteristic of moorland and form the basis of peat, which is semi-fossilized plant material, sufficiently old to be burnt as a fuel. Often moors are created by felling forests. Once trees have gone, soil erosion and exposure make regrowth difficult, especially where deer or sheep are grazing. Heathers are the most striking plants, covering the rolling scenery in an endless sheet of purple flowers in late summer. Earlier in the year, bright yellow gorse will have been prominent, and in autumn berries form on various types of blueberry, valuable food for both birds and mammals.

This is exposed country, cold, wet and windy. Animal life is scarce, but hares and red deer find enough to eat, as do grouse. These gamebirds flourish on heather shoots. With wonderfully camouflaged plumage, they spend most of their lives on the ground, tak-

HEAVIEST ANTELOPE IS ELAND AT 900 kg, SMALLEST IS ROYAL AT 3 kg

Below: Heathland supports many unusual plants and animals.

WOODCHAT SHRIKE

SUBALPINE WARBLER

Above: The gerenuk can eat tender shoots out of reach of other scrubland antelopes.

HORNET

ing flight only when danger is very close, when they whirr away at speed low over the moor. Moorland hunters include hen harriers, which glide on stiffly held wings a couple of metres above the heather, relying on surprise and a sudden pounce to catch unsuspecting small animal prey.

Downland

Gently rolling chalk or limestone hills, covered in a thin layer of soil, are the basis of downs. A few bushes of hawthorn and juniper survive grazing rabbits and sheep. Plant life is dominated by grasses, which shelter chalk-tolerant specialist plants such as the aromatic thymes, rock roses (now widely grown in rock gardens), and orchids. In temperate climates, chalk downland is the best orchid habitat, particularly for those such as bee, butterfly, spider and fly named after the animals their flowers imitate.

Open-land birds such as skylarks and pipits predominate, with the specialist stone-curlew. This strange wader nests far from the shore on dry downland, and is also locally called "thick-knee" because of the knobbly joint in the middle of its long legs, which looks as if it should be the knee but bends the wrong way and is actually its ankle. Huge eyes give a clue to

the stone-curlews' nocturnal life style. They hunt small soil animals and will even eat lizards and voles. Their weird shrieking calls shatter the peace of moonlit downland nights.

Scrubland

Various grassy habitats with plenty of bushes and herbaceous plants are called scrub. Often the bushes are thorny like gorse and blackberry, well protected against grazing animals. In warm climates near the Mediterranean, many plants are either extremely prickly or powerfully pungent, and this defence strategy is effective even against hungry goats. On the plains of Africa, most plants are either strongly aromatic, or have an irritant or poisonous white latex sap. Many acacias have thorns 5 cm long, as sharp and strong as a nail and just as capable of puncturing the tyre of an all-terrain vehicle. This defence is only partly successful against hungry giraffes and antelopes, which insert long tongues or pointed noses between the thorns to secure a meal of tender leaves.

60 MILLION BISON ROAMED USA • ARMADILLO HAS UNIQUE BONE PLATE ARMOUR

LIFE AMONG THE TREES

Woodlands vary greatly around the world. In Australia, eucalyptus are the commonest trees, while in the tropical climate around the equator jungle and rainforest predominate (p. 44). Boreal forests lie close to the Arctic Circle, mixtures of short-needled evergreen conifers such as spruce with clusters of birch and aspen. Beneath the forest canopy of leaves, deep shade limits the number of plants that can survive, and flowering plants flourish far better around woodland edges and in glades and clearings.

Conifer Specialists

Cones provide a valuable food source for squirrels, and for their predators, the pine martens, forest equivalent to the stoats of open country. Crested tits and azure-winged magpies also flourish in pine woods, but *the* specialist birds of this habitat are crossbills. Crossbills are finches with strong parrot-like beaks, with the beak tips crossed over, an adaptation which allows them to extract the seeds from deep inside pine cones. Two-barred crossbills have lightweight beaks and can handle flimsy spruce cones, while the massive beak of the parrot crossbill has evolved to tackle the much stronger cones of pines.

Winter Survival

Temperate-woodland mammals range in size from the huge elk or moose of the far north, and red, fallow and roe deer which are far more widely distributed, through wolves, bears and wild boar (all sadly depleted in numbers by hunters in any but the biggest forests), down to squirrels and small rodents.

In deciduous woods, squirrels, boar and dormice show wonderfully contrasting solutions to the problems of surviving the winter. All find plenty of food during the summer, but come under pressure in autumn as plants prepare for winter. Squirrels collect hundreds of acorns from oaks, and cache them, buried in the soil. Later in winter, with the ground covered in snow, a hungry squirrel will leave the shel-

Right: Man is rapidly replacing broadleaved deciduous forests with conifer plantations.

PURPLE EMPEROR

SPANGLE GALLS

DORMOUSE

GREY SQUIRREL

450 SPECIES OF OAK WORLDWIDE • 2,000 DIFFERENT INSECTS LIVE ON OAK TREES

Left: Forest oaks provide food or a home for a tremendous range of plants and animals. Lichens live on the bark, and fungi on decaying wood.

CHIFFCHAFF

WOODPECKER

STAG BEETLE

ter of its drey and find almost all its hidden food. Wild boars are much larger, and gorge on the abundance of autumn acorns, growing fat in the process. They use this fat as an emergency food store, and as insulation, but are big and have strong enough noses to dig up roots and bulbs even from frozen soil. Squirrels cannot risk getting too fat, or they would not be fast enough to escape from predatory hawks. Boars do not have this problem. Tiny dormice are unusual mammals that truly hibernate. In autumn, they feed on berries and nuts, and get very fat. They build sheltered nests of leaves, curl up and go to sleep – for four or five months! To save energy so that fat reserves last, hibernating dormice let their body temperature drop to a few degrees above freezing, and their pulse and breathing are barely detectable.

Woodland Carpenters

Woodpeckers have loud calls and drum with their beaks on resonating dead branches, good ways of making contact in dense woodland habitat. As their name suggests, woodpeckers get their food by using their heads and beaks as a combination hammer and chisel, prizing away flakes of wood to reach the tunnels of wood-boring insects. Once in, they use a tongue several centimetres long to reach the grub. The tongue has a horny tip shaped like a harpoon, and stabs the grub, dragging it out to be eaten. When not in use, the enormous tongue, rather than overfilling the bird's mouth, lives in a special tubular sheath that runs down the woodpecker's neck before doing a U-turn and finishing up coiled on top of its skull. An elastic pad of cartilage between beak and skull prevents woodpeckers getting brain damage or headaches while excavating their nest holes in tree trunks.

JUNGLES

Tropical forests still cover about 10 per cent of the earth's surface, but each year large areas are cut down and not replanted. Amazingly, 2,500 million people, about half the world population, live in poorly developed tropical-jungle countries and still use wood for cooking. Although they chop down trees for firewood, and slash and burn forest clearings to plant crops for a few years, local tribespeople cause much less damage than national or international companies seeking valuable forest products. Besides expensive timbers such as teak and mahogany – popular for furniture-making in the more developed countries of the world – these include latex sap that produces natural rubber, fruit such as bananas, coffee beans and cocoa pods, palm oils, and such medicines as everyday aspirin and the quinine vital in treating malaria.

Jungle trees have tall trunks, reaching 70 m above the forest floor. To give them extra strength they have flanges at their bases called buttresses, similar to the stonework supports that help hold up the walls of old cathedrals. Often there is little vegetation on the ground because only 1 per cent of the sunlight penetrates the thick leafy canopy.

Perching Plants

Obviously, up in the canopy there is no soil for smaller plants to root in, but whole families have developed treetop life styles as epiphytes. Epiphytes use some of their roots to anchor themselves to the rough bark of these monster trees, while other roots dangle free to absorb vital moisture from the jungle air. As it rains almost every day, with between 200 and 500 cm falling each year, the air beneath the canopy is often very humid. Many spectacular tropical orchids perch on trees, as do most members of the bromeliad family. Bromeliads have wide fleshy leaves that collect rainwater where they meet the stem, deep enough to provide a mini-pond habitat, far above ground, for aquatic insects and tree frogs.

Tiny but Toxic

Tree frogs are often only a couple of centimetres long, and many are green, well camouflaged against the canopy leaves. Much of the eerie noise resounding through jungles after dark comes from their tiny throats. Others are strikingly coloured, often red, blue or yellow and black. These are arrow-poison

ANTEATER'S TONGUE 60 cm LONG

frogs. Their colours should warn other creatures that they are either dangerous, or taste unpleasant. Forest Indian tribes many centuries ago found that some are extremely poisonous. Before they go hunting, or fight with neighbouring tribes, they dip the tips of their arrows in a brew of this poison mixed with plant sap.

Jungle Acrobats

Parrots are common in jungles. They are fruit-eaters, and the agility that unfortunately makes them popular pets is of great help as they clamber about in the canopy. They can perch gripping with one powerful foot, holding a fig up to their mouths like an ice-cream in the other and extracting its juicy contents with their hooked beaks. Many parrots are brightly coloured, particularly the macaws of South America. Black, blue, or scarlet and yellow, they measure almost 1 m from beak to tail tip. They raise their young in holes in forest trees, feeding them only on fruit as other foods are scarce. Fruit is not the most nutritious diet, and young macaws are 12 weeks or more growing in the nest, compared with the four or five weeks for other birds of similar size but fed a mixed diet with a higher protein content.

Above: Startling colours warn predators that arrow-poison frogs have poisonous glands in their skin.

Left and right: Dense tropical rainforests contain a huge array of fascinating and often colourful wildlife.

SLOTHS MOVE AT ONLY 1 km/h

LIFE IN DESERTS

Above: Crescent-shaped dunes are characteristic of sandy deserts.

Geographers identify about 20 per cent of the world's surface as desert, where less than 25 cm of rain falls each year. This is an average figure, and in many desert areas no rain may fall for several years, and what does fall may come during just two or three storms. One part of the Atacama of Chile had no rain at all for 400 years. Some deserts are huge, like the Sahara in north Africa which covers almost 10 million sq km. Most deserts are largely rocky, or covered in gravel or pebbles, but some are composed of huge sand dunes which may shift up to 50 m in a year, blown by the wind, swallowing up oases in their path.

The Gobi and American deserts are "cold" deserts, with seasonal differences between extremely hot summers and very cold winters. The Sahara, Kalahari and Australian deserts are "hot" because they are extremely hot all day, year-round. In "hot" deserts, daytime temperatures often exceed 50 °C, but at night temperatures often drop to freezing point.

Life at the Limit

Lack of water, extreme heat during the day and cold at night, with rock, gravel or sand offering little op-portunity for root development, make deserts extremely difficult places for plants to grow. Two very different forms of plant life have evolved to cope with this. One type is composed of specialist annual plants with extremely short active lives. Following sudden rains, these plant seeds germinate very quickly, and the plants grow equally fast while the water lasts. They flower, and soon set seed which ripens rapidly in the hot sun. The plants die as water runs out, seeds falling to the ground. There they remain, thick-skinned and almost moistureless, resistant to drought conditions, often lying for many years until rain falls again and their hasty life cycle restarts.

Cacti, native only to America, have evolved another tactic. Leaves are reduced to sharp spines for protection against grazing animals, while the swollen green stem serves both to photosynthesize food for growth and as a store for water over the months when none is available as rain.

Amazingly, some animals manage to survive these harsh conditions, sheltering down holes or under rocks to escape the heat of the day, emerging at night to feed. Insects tolerate these conditions better than most, and the ant-lion even turns the loose sand to its advantage. Ant-lions are the larvae of insects related to lacewings. They dig a conical pit in the sand, burying themselves at the bottom. Unwary insects come

HOTTEST SPOT ON EARTH DEATH VALLEY, CALIFORNIA, AT 80 °C

MASTER MIGRANTS

Of all animals, birds are the masters of migration, helped by their powers of flight. Like other migrants, some birds seek to escape from winter snow, which stops them feeding and could starve them to death. Others fly half way around the world to breed and enjoy the brief arctic summer when food is plentiful. Champions among these are the arctic terns. They breed north of the Arctic Circle, and in autumn fly south past Europe, over the equator and past Africa to the Antarctic Ocean, just off the ice floes. But this is the antarctic summer, so food is plentiful and living easy. Some arctic terns live for more than 20 years, and, flying almost from pole to pole twice each year, their lifetime mileage will exceed 1 million km! As they breed in the arctic summer, when the sun shines almost all day, and spend the rest of the year in the antarctic summer, again with 24 hours of sunlight daily, they see more sun in their lifetime than any other creature. Although migrants are able to navigate with pinpoint accuracy, using the stars, sun and moon, and can correct their course to allow for crosswinds, just how they manage to do this with such precision is still largely a mystery.

Below: A numbered ring is fitted to the leg of a sharp-shinned hawk. Reports of ringed birds tell us much about their migratory routes.

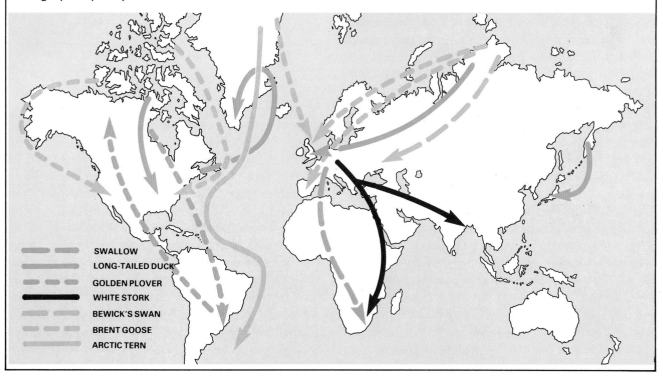

- — — SWALLOW
- — — LONG-TAILED DUCK
- — — GOLDEN PLOVER
- ▬▬ WHITE STORK
- — — BEWICK'S SWAN
- — — BRENT GOOSE
- — — ARCTIC TERN

PRONGHORN ANTELOPES CAN GALLOP AT 50 km/h FOR MANY HOURS

SPREADING THEMSELVES

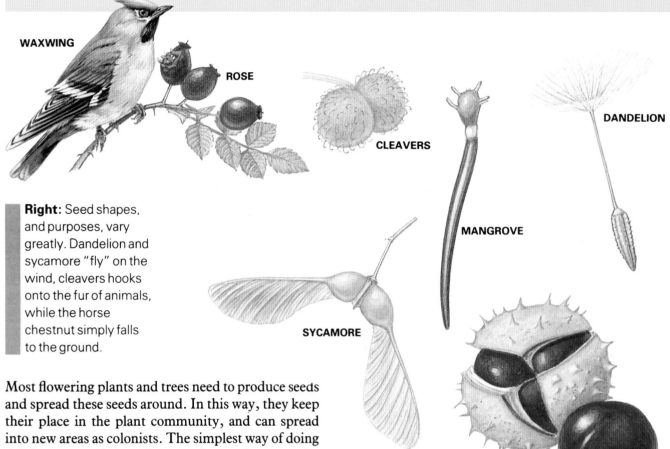

WAXWING

ROSE

CLEAVERS

MANGROVE

DANDELION

SYCAMORE

HORSE
CHESTNUT

Right: Seed shapes, and purposes, vary greatly. Dandelion and sycamore "fly" on the wind, cleavers hooks onto the fur of animals, while the horse chestnut simply falls to the ground.

Most flowering plants and trees need to produce seeds and spread these seeds around. In this way, they keep their place in the plant community, and can spread into new areas as colonists. The simplest way of doing this is to set seeds in a cluster or in a pod, as peas do, and to let them drop when ripe into the soil beneath the plant. Balsams set their seeds in an explosive pod. When it is touched, the ripe pod splits open suddenly and twists. This sends the seeds flying for about 2 m, and has earned the plant the name "touch-me-not". This sort of seed can be quite large and heavy: horse chestnut conkers, for example, are often 30 mm across and weigh over 30 g. They can carry good food stores to help the germinating seedling over its difficult first few days.

Carried by the Waves

Coconuts fall off their palm tree onto the beach, and despite their weight they may be washed away by the sea and float hundreds of kilometres to a fresh tropical island. The dart-shaped fruit of the mangrove also drifts around in the sea. When it washes ashore and the tide falls, the point at one end sticks in the soft mud. This gives the seed an anchor so that it can put out a root and shoot quickly, before stormy weather can uproot it.

Using the Wind

Other seeds travel long distances, but use the wind. Some, such as ash, sycamore and hornbeam, are heavy seeds with good food stores, but have a sail or blade attached. As they fall, this sail acts like a helicopter rotor, slowing the drop and allowing them to travel many metres and disperse from the parent tree with some assistance from the wind.

Some windborne seeds are shaped like parachutes. Dandelion seeds, for example, are quite big, which slows down their spread by the wind. Other seeds, such as those of thistles and willowherbs, have long plumes or tufts of lightweight down that act as sails. These may carry them for many kilometres before touchdown. Fireweed, which is related to the willowherbs, probably blew across the Atlantic Ocean

FUNGUS PILOBOLUS FIRES SPORES 30 cm • CONVOLVULUS CAN SPREAD 10 m A YEAR

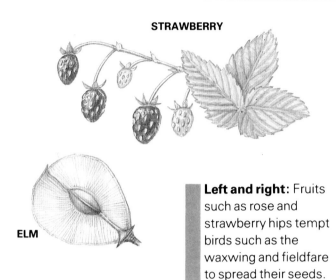

STRAWBERRY

ELM

Left and right: Fruits such as rose and strawberry hips tempt birds such as the waxwing and fieldfare to spread their seeds.

from the USA to colonize Europe. For the plants, the disadvantage is that the seeds must be very light. They can carry little food reserve and must germinate and root quickly if they are to survive.

Hitching a Lift

Cleavers, or goose grass, is a wonderful example of seeds that hitch lifts. The seed coat is covered in masses of tiny hooks which cling to the fur of a passing animal, to be knocked off or cleaned off some distance away. It was from such seeds that an inventor got the idea for velcro fastenings. We may spread seeds accidentally, too, on muddy tractor wheels, or even between countries far apart when wild-plant seeds travel mixed up with the seeds of crops such as wheat.

It may seem odd, but it is good for some plants to have their fruit eaten by birds. Brightly coloured sweet fruits are eagerly eaten by hungry birds, and, so long as the seed is tough enough not to be digested, the bird may fly a long distance before the seed passes out in its droppings.

But not all plants set seed – at least not always. Many, like strawberries, spread amazingly quickly by runners or suckers, budding off plantlets that take root close by. Even these plants must rely on seeds when the going gets tough. During droughts, floods or severe frosts, strawberry plants and their runners could easily be killed, but the seeds on the strawberry fruit can survive these hazards to give rise to a fresh generation of plants.

Below: Some mangrove seeds germinate before they leave the parent plant. They drop and almost at once take root in the mud.

MANGROVE

MUD SKIPPER

MANGROVE SEED

HUMMINGBIRDS CARRY POLLEN FROM ONE HIBISCUS PLANT TO ANOTHER

ANIMAL HOMES

Human builders work with great precision. Paths are level, walls vertical, bricks are laid in straight lines and neatly interlocked for extra strength. The skills of builders ensure this, backed up by tools ranging from excavators and power drills to hammers and spirit levels. In nature, no such technological aids are available, yet many of the structures built by animals have all the strength and security of human homes.

Paper Castles

In spring, queen wasps emerge from hibernation and start to build new colonies. Choosing a sheltered spot in a roof, hole in the ground or hollow tree, they construct a spherical nest. Queens collect and chew wood fibre, often from fenceposts, and use it mixed with saliva as we use papier mâché. Paper-thin but rigid, nests start off at golf-ball size and can grow as big as footballs. Inside the spherical casing are rows of six-sided cells neatly interlocked, which give extra strength to the nest. We use a similar hexagonal light-weight cellular reinforcement to strengthen doors and the metal skins of aircraft.

Bricklayers

Some birds use bricks just as we do. Swallows and house martins collect pellets of mud in their beaks from puddle edges, mixing them with a few bits of straw before laying them neatly in rows around the walls of their cup-shaped nests. In Arab and Asian countries, village houses are still made from mud bricks reinforced with straw and allowed to dry in the sun, just like a martin's nest.

Masterbuilders

Although birds are expert flyers, their powers of flight were gained during evolution only at the expense of some losses. As their "arms" became wings with feathers, they lost the use of their hands, a situation we would find impossible. Despite this, birds are among the masterbuilders, using just their beaks and feet to do the delicate work. Long-tailed tits build pouch-shaped nests deep in thorny thickets. Long animal hairs and spiders' webs are the main structural materials, with moss and feathers woven in for warmth and insulation. A single nest may contain 2,000 feathers, each carried in on a separate flight.

Most expert of all are the African weaver birds.

AFRICAN HAMMERHEAD STORKS BUILD 0.5-TONNE STICK-AND-MUD NESTS IN TREES

Male palm weavers build hanging basket nests woven from torn-off strips of palm leaf. Tying these onto a palm frond, they weave other strips into place, tying down where necessary and using just beak and feet. The nests have an entrance tunnel, and hang free, safe from predatory snakes and lizards and enjoying breezes to cool the burning heat of the African sun.

Major Engineering Works

Beavers are the engineers of the animal world. By building dams across streams, they can actually change the landscape in which they live by creating lakes and swamps. Their dams are massive barriers of

Below: Beavers dam rivers to provide a safe place to build the "lodge" where they sleep and give birth.

Above: The massive tenement nest of a colony of social weavers dwarfs the tree supporting it.

branches and logs, with many logs several centimetres in diameter. These are expertly felled by beavers using their huge front teeth, which have hard brown enamel in front and softer white enamel behind. These grow continuously to allow for such heavy use, but do not wear down evenly, as the harder brown enamel lasts longer and gives the teeth a sharp and effective chisel shape. Deep in the heart of the dam is the lodge, the beavers' living quarters. Usually this has an underground entrance that deters most predators but which beavers, expert swimmers, can use easily. If danger threatens, they slap the water with their flat tails and swim for cover.

TERMITE MOUNDS 6 m ABOVE AND BELOW GROUND • LONGEST BEAVER DAM 700 m

ANIMAL HUNTERS

Hunting is one of the most specialized ways that an animal can live, and animal hunting skills compare favourably with anything that human technology has developed, even in this age of sophisticated weaponry. A leopard, creeping like a snake and almost invisible despite it size, can approach its unsuspecting prey far more stealthily than a commando. Like most members of the cat family, leopards have relatively slim but muscular hind legs which provide the power for a sprint to catch their prey by surprise, and strong front legs with massive claws to wrestle it to the ground. Then a powerful bite from huge canine teeth seals the victim's fate.

Teamwork

Prides of lions often hunt in cooperation, some members of the team driving their prey into an ambush set by the others. Wolves are prepared for much longer chases, taking turns at running in the lead, snapping at the heels of the caribou they are hunting until it turns at bay. They use a team discipline that would be the envy of soldiers.

Masters of Their Element

Great white sharks are 6-m-long, perfectly streamlined torpedoes of solid muscle power. These oceanic super-predators are guided by a superb sense of taste that can scent blood several kilometres away, and have an amazing ability to detect and identify movements in the water even as small as a heartbeat. Their normal prey is seals and turtles, so it is easy to see how they

Above: Most feared of all ocean predators, a great white shark patrols on the alert for prey.

PEREGRINES DIVE ON PREY AT 200 km/h • LITTLE OWLS KILL PREY TWICE OWN WEIGHT

Above: Not all cheetah hunts result in a kill. When it is successful, the cheetah may be robbed by stronger lions or hyaenas, so it must drag its prey to hide it in long grass.

can occasionally mistakenly attack a human swimmer paddling his surfboard out to sea, and turn into man-eaters. Their fearsome array of sharp triangular teeth are pushed forward as the jaws open and the shark powers in to the attack, and can easily chop the swimmer and surfboard in half.

Small but Devastating

But not all hunters are large. One microscopic roundworm hunter, less than 1 mm long, has been enlisted by farmers to help in pest control. These roundworms are parasites of weevil larvae that badly damage plant roots. Moving through the soil, roundworms seek their victim like an Exocet missile by following the faintest of chemical clues to its hideout. Once they have tracked it down, they pierce its skin and release toxic bacteria which they carry like a warhead. This quickly immobilizes the weevil, and saves a great deal of harmful pesticide pollution of farmland.

Prey on the Lookout

If animal hunters have special features, so, too, do their prey. For them, the most important thing is to escape alive. The simplest way is to be always watchful, with excellent sight and hearing to give warning of approaching danger. Live in a flock or herd, and many pairs of alert eyes and ears combined give everyone better protection. There are more bizarre ways of escaping. An American possum caught by a coyote goes limp and "plays dead", hoping that its captor will lose interest and drop it, and off it runs. Ringed plovers, protecting their eggs or chicks, run along just in front of predatory crows, trailing one wing as if it were broken. This distracts the hunter, who turns to chase the adult bird, which flies off in the nick of time.

The ultimate deterrent weapon is held by the skunk. Should a cougar threaten, the skunk raises its fluffy tail. If the cougar takes no notice and attacks, the skunk squirts out a jet of foul-smelling fluid, so awful that the cougar turns and runs away.

Left: In a pride of lions, it is usually the females who do the hunting. They often use teamwork to catch and kill an antelope.

GIANT ANTEATERS HAVE TONGUES 60 cm LONG, AND EAT 30,000 ANTS DAILY

PLANTS AS HUNTERS

It seems strange to think of plants as hunters or predators, but many plants live at least partly off other plants or animals. Most green (or greenish) plants make their own food using the sun's energy and the special chemical chlorophyll (p. 16). But some plant groups, such as the fungi, lack this green chlorophyll pigment and are often whitish or brownish in colour. They get their food by fastening on to some other organism, sometimes alive but more often dead.

Above: Sticky glandular hairs glistening, the sundew plant awaits insects unwary enough to be attracted to it.

Clearing up the Debris

If the fungus is feeding on an animal or plant that is already dead or dying, we call it a saprophyte. Saprophytes are tremendously helpful in assisting in decay and rotting, which returns the vital chemicals locked up in plant and animal bodies to the soil so that they can be used again. Only with the help of saprophyte fungi and bacteria recycling dead waste material can life continue on earth.

Harmful Plants

When the plant or animal attacked is alive, we call the fungus a parasite, and parasites are usually harmful to their host. Most fungi have a mass of root-like threads called hyphae that absorb food and water. In parasites, the hyphae penetrate the host cells and absorb the cell contents, which are rich in food. Many fungus parasites do not cause much damage, but others, such as honey fungus and Dutch elm disease, can quickly kill even huge trees.

Some parasitic fungi will even attack us. Athlete's foot, a painful itching between the toes, is caused by fungus feeding on our skin in the ideal moist habitat we offer if we do not dry our feet properly. Others we can actually use to help us by killing harmful insects.

Below: *Rafflesia* derives its food from dead or dying plant roots. Pitcher plants are carnivorous, trapping unwary insects.

PARASITIC FUNGUS ARMILLARIA KILLS MATURE TREES IN 2 YEARS

Farmers spray their crops with a fungus that attacks aphids. This saves using chemical pesticides that would damage the whole environment, and is called biological control. Some flowering plants work in the same way as the fungi. Broomrapes and dodder extend root-like tubes into the cells of other plants to extract the sap, letting the other plant do all the hard work of making food for them both.

Hunting Plants

Plants growing in habitats where some natural nutrients are in short supply must find alternative means of obtaining them. In tropical jungles, where the soil is made mostly of decaying leaves, with all the goodness washed out by heavy rains, pitcher plants make up for the missing items in their diet by catching insects. Some of their leaves are specially modified to look like pitchers or jugs. Inside is a sugar solution that acts as a bait for insects. They climb over the lip of the pitcher, slide down the slippery surface and cannot get out again. The sugary bait also contains digestive juices which slowly dissolve the insects and allow the pitcher plant to use the chemical components.

Other predatory plants use different kinds of traps. Sundew leaves are covered in tiny club-shaped sticky

RAFFLESIA

Above right: Broomrapes feed on other plants. Their "roots" are not in soil, but embedded deep in the roots of their host.

hairs. These trap wandering spiders and beetles, and flies tempted by their shiny sugary appearance. Once stuck to one hair, struggling insects are soon entangled on others. The leaf produces juices which slowly digest the prey, releasing tiny quantities of chemicals needed by sundews to grow and flower.

Venus's fly trap has hinged leaves with stiff spines around the edges. Should an unwary fly land on the leaf, it will touch sensitive trigger hairs and the leaf will snap shut like an old-fashioned man trap.

PITCHER PLANT

FUNGUS CARRYING DUTCH ELM DISEASE IS SPREAD BY WOOD-BORING BEETLES

COMMUNICATION

Animal lives are full of signals, picked up by the senses and decoded by the brain, which issues instructions through the nervous system on what to do or not to do. To humans, a red light or the referee's whistle means "stop", while a green light means "go". The noise from the dry-skin rattle at the tip of a cornered rattlesnake's tail sounds a warning that is equally clearly understood.

To be greeted with a smile means that a person is friendly, and many animals rely on similar body language to convey messages. Dominant hyaenas show they know their own strength by raising the fur hackles on their neck and shoulders. Other hyaenas show they know who is boss by cowering with their heads low and with their lips curled back to show their teeth in a submissive, "want-to-be-friends" smile.

Voice Messages

Male blackbirds use their musical songs to attract females, partly by the rich variety of notes the song contains, and perhaps partly by messages coded into those notes. Song is also used to tell other blackbirds to keep away from their territory, where they will nest and raise a family. Birds' hearing is far better than ours, and playing a birdsong recording at one-eighth speed shows just what complex messages birds can send by voice.

Sailors in the days of sailing ships knew that whales could sing. Larger whales produce groans and grunts,

Right: Zebra stripes have many purposes: in the open, the animals can see each other; in dappled shade stripes provide camouflage; and their flashing can confuse predators.

DOLPHINS USE OVER 30 SOUNDS • WHALE SONGS MAY LAST 24 HOURS

Right: A complex "dance" pattern performed by worker bees returning to the hive tells other bees the direction to fly in to find a rich source of nectar or pollen.

while smaller dolphins and porpoises produce pings, whistles and clicks. Low sounds travel further in water than in air, and the song-like messages of humpbacks can be heard by other whales an astonishing several hundred kilometres away.

Visual Signals

Animals use colours for various purposes. Male birds of paradise are the most colourful and exotic of all birds. Most have feathers of several brilliant hues, sparkling with reflected light like thousands of tiny mirrors. With plumes fluffed out, groups of males hang upside down from branches, shaking their feathers so that they resemble coloured waterfalls. This

brilliant display attracts females, who watch quietly before flying off with the male of their choice.

At first sight, the striped coats of zebras seem to make them look conspicuous. Stripes have several uses. Every zebra has a different face pattern, so each can be recognized by other zebras. When the herd is grazing safely, the stripes are all lined up and conspicuous, so no zebra loses sight of its friends. But if danger such as a hunting lion threatens, zebras gallop off in all directions. The stripes become jumbled up, dazzling and confusing the lion and making it difficult to choose a target zebra and make a kill.

Insects such as wasps, with poisonous bites or stings, usually have brightly patterned bodies, warning predatory birds that they are dangerous and should be avoided. Hoverflies and some other insects that actually have no bite or sting imitate wasp colours and fool predators into thinking that they are dangerous, and so are left well alone.

Glow worms attract their mates by using light that they generate themselves. Glow worms are actually beetles, and it is the wingless females which produce the light by mixing two chemicals, luciferin and luciferase, from glands in their tails. Combined in air, these chemicals produce a cold greenish-white light, bright enough to attract males from several metres away, and bright enough to be used as bedside lights by children in days before electric light. A few glow worms in a jar were less dangerous than a candle and far brighter to read by.

RHINOCEROSES USE PILES OF DUNG AND SPRAY URINE ON BUSHES TO MARK TERRITORIES

ANIMAL SENSES

All creatures, including ourselves, need a continuously updated supply of information about what is going on in our environment. All animals need to recognize their food, and to distinguish nutritious from harmful. Hunters need to know where their prey is, and how fast in which direction they need to move to catch it, which is the sort of information that on-board computers on jet fighters supply. Eyes, ears and nose are usually the main guides to the hunter, just as they are for those animals that are the prey of others, where the senses need to be specially alert for escaping when danger threatens.

Sight and Sound

Owls out hunting after dark also have wonderful sight. They have such huge eyes that they cannot swivel in their sockets, but instead owls must turn their whole head. Their sharpest sense, however, is not sight, but hearing. Owl feathers are generally velvet-soft for silent flight, but the feathers of the disc surrounding the face are much stiffer. This disc serves as a reflector, collecting the faintest of sounds and focusing them into the owl's huge ears, which are tucked away behind the feathers, just as a receiver dish collects and focuses TV signals from satellite broadcasts. In total darkness, a hunting long-eared owl can detect and pinpoint a scuffling mouse 20 m away, and launch off on silent wings to strike with its fearsome talons.

Bats also hunt after dark, but they have very poor eyesight. Their strangely ugly bulbous noses emit streams of high-pitched squeaks. These bounce off objects in the bats' flight path, and the echoes are picked up by their fleshy leaf-like ears. So acute is their echo-location system that their brains can decode the signals received and identify dangerous twigs or wires that must be dodged, or insect prey that should be chased, caught and eaten.

On the Scent

Dogs called pointers are used by human hunters to find gamebirds. Once they have picked up the scent, they line up their long nose, back and stiffly held tail pointing straight at where the bird is hiding. This is far better than humans could manage with their very poor sense of smell, but, of all animals, moths must be among the best at smelling. Female moths, which

ANEMONE

SPONGE

SIMPLE ANIMALS

Encrusting sponges (left) have very simple sensory systems. The sea anemone, although still a simple animal, has more sophisticated sensors alerting it to prey, firing poison darts to paralyse its victim.

A DOG'S SENSE OF SMELL IS A MILLION TIMES BETTER THAN A HUMAN'S

Left: Its huge ears receiving the echo-location signals bouncing off its prey, a false vampire bat swoops in to strike an unsuspecting mouse.

Right: The green tree snake catches insects and lizards using its sense of smell and by detecting their vibrations.

have simple club-shaped antennae, give out special scents called pheromones to attract males. Using their much more complicated fern-like antennae, some male moths can detect a female over 2 km away.

Super Senses

Snakes are shortsighted, and have poor hearing, being better at sensing vibrations through the ground. They rely most on their sense of smell, but scent particles are not detected in the same way as they are by other animals. Instead, each time the forked tongue flicks in and out, it collects scent particles on its moist surface. These are carried to special pits in the roof of the snake's mouth called Jacobsen's organs, and identified. Hunting snakes flick their tongues in and out even faster to get as much information on their prey and its movements as possible. Some snakes, called pit vipers, have heat-sensitive pits on their cheeks. After dark and even underground, these can detect the body warmth of potential prey such as rats or mice, and give the viper accurate enough information to allow it to strike, injecting a lethal dose of venom through its curved fangs.

Below: Excellent powers of sight allow vultures from miles around to gather at a carcass with quite amazing speed.

WADING BIRDS IDENTIFY FOOD IN MUD WITH NERVES ON THEIR BEAK TIPS

PLANT MESSAGES

Unlike animals, plants have no complex network of nerves, controlled by a central brain, receiving information from millions of sensory nerve endings before sending out nerve messages to the body muscles telling them to make an appropriate response. Instead, their growth and their rather slow responses to changes in their environment are usually governed by chemical "messengers" called hormones. These hormones are made by the cells in one part of the plant – it may be a leaf, or the growing tip of a root or shoot – and are sent through the sap to convey instructions to cells in other parts. Two hormones may act in tandem, one slowing down the changes caused by the other.

Chemical Control

Hormones called auxins are produced by the cells near the shoot tip. They help start off root growth, and cause stem cells to grow in length. Auxins also produce movements of shoots and flowers. All the flowerheads in a field of sunflowers turn during the day so that the full face of the flower is always exposed to the warmth of the sun. This is called phototropism, and helps make the flowers attractive to pollinating insects; later in the year, it helps to ripen the seeds. Turning happens when auxins are diverted to the shaded side of the stem. They stimulate faster growth in the shaded cells than in those in the sun, and so bend the stem and flower towards the sunlight.

Right: Although slower in reaction time than most animals, sunflower senses allow their ripening seeds to follow the hot sun.

Cytokinins in the shoot tip control the multiplication rate of cells there. High cytokinin levels increase cell division, so the shoot tip grows away faster. Other hormones produced by the shoot-tip cells act over shorter distances to stop side buds from forming. This is called apical dominance and allows the leading bud to develop without harmful crowding and competition from a cluster of side shoots. This effect fades further away from the shoot tip, and, once the hormones are too dilute to be effective, side buds develop and branches eventually form.

Sunlight is vital for green plant growth, but its effects on the shoot-tip cells are important in flowering. Light-sensitive chemicals (photoreceptors) in the cells measure daylength. Some plants such as *Nicotiana* and *Petunia* flower only when daylight hours are long, while others such as cultivated *Chrysanthemum* flower

A GERMINATING BEAN SEED

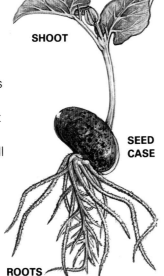

SHOOT

Right: Having had its growth triggered by detecting the correct conditions, the germinating seed will grow upwards and towards light.

SEED CASE

ROOTS

LIGHT-SENSITIVE CHEMICAL PHYTOCHROME ALLOWS PLANT TO TELL TIME OF DAY

to reduce the size of cherry trees. Once 25 m high, many are now only 5 m and much easier for picking.

Deciduous trees shed their leaves in autumn, a hormone called abscissic acid carrying the chemical instructions to leaf bases, sealing off phloem and xylem vessels and building a layer of corky cells where leaves can break off without damaging the tree. A similar process isolates apples from the rest of the tree when they are ready to fall.

Handle with Care

Sensitive plants, members of the *Mimosa* family, move surprisingly swiftly by changing the water content of special cells where the leaflets join the midrib. If these cells are touched or shaken, they lose water rapidly and the leaflets droop, often closing the leaf up.

Right: The "sensitive plant", the *Mimosa*, reacts to touch far more quickly than most plants.

when daylength is short. Nurserymen can manipulate flowering seasons by keeping plants in greenhouses with either too much or too little light for flowering hormones to be produced. When they want plants to flower, they adjust the daylength to bring the crop into flower.

Hormones are also used artificially to help difficult cuttings to root, and they are particularly useful for inducing increases in the size of dwarf plants. Fruit-growers use man-made hormones in the opposite way.

PLANT LEAVES TURN TO FOLLOW PATH OF SUN TO MAXIMIZE LIGHT RECEPTION

ANIMAL MOVEMENT

Most animals have been shaped by millions of years of evolution to move as efficiently as possible to suit their life style and their particular environment.

On Land

Snails may have only one foot, but for the animals' size their feet are among the biggest in the animal kingdom. Even with a heavy shell to carry, snails can cross rough ground, move along prickly branches, and even climb up sheets of glass. The foot is muscular but flexible, and the sole works like a suction cup on smooth

Right: Kangaroos' prodigious leaps, powered by elastic tendons and balanced by the tail, are an energy-efficient way of travelling at speed.

surfaces. The secret of a travelling snail is its trail of slime, secreted by the sole. This lubricates the way over rough rocks, or like thick grease acts as an adhesive, helping snails climb vertical surfaces.

Slimline snakes are able to hunt prey down holes where limbs would get in the way, but even without limbs they move very effectively. They actually walk on the ends of their ribs, as each rib moves one of the scales on the snake's belly. In turn, one scale is moved a little way forward to take a fresh grip, then the next, and so on. By shaping their bodies in an S, snakes can climb trees and even move across desert sand dunes at astonishing speed.

Cheetahs still have all five toes, and are the fastest land animals. Deer and antelope have only two toes remaining on each foot, and horses only one. The horse's hoof is the equivalent of the nail on the human middle (and longest) finger. The other toes have shrunk to become strengthening and supporting bones. Deer, antelope, and horses have been timed at 70 km/h, compared with the cheetah's 115 km/h.

ACROBATIC GIBBONS CAN SWING FROM ONE BRANCH TO ANOTHER 12 m AWAY

Leaps and Bounds

Jumping animals usually make one leap at a time, pausing after each leap to get their legs ready for the next. Kangaroos are different: balanced by their large, heavy tail, they bound non-stop across the Australian outback. Each leap covers 12 m, because, inside the legs, elastic tendons work like powerful springs so that kangaroos actually bounce along. This is one of the most energy-saving ways of getting around in the whole animal kingdom.

Up in the Trees

As most monkeys move like acrobats through the treetops, they use their tails to help. In Africa and Asia, tails help the monkeys to balance, but South American monkeys have prehensile tails, where the tail tip can coil around a branch and give support like an extra hand and arm, strong enough to support the swinging monkey's weight.

At the slow end of life in the treetops is the sloth. Most of their lives sloths hang upside down, munching leaves for food and spending 15 hours each day asleep. They move so slowly that, in the damp jungle, mosses and lichens have time to grow on their fur.

Above: This peregrine falcon has its rock dove prey secured in mid-air after a 200-km/h dive.

Beneath the Sea

Fish propel themselves through the water by continuous snake-like S movements of their muscular bodies, with the tail sweeping from side to side. Marine mammals such as the whales and seals have horizontal tail fins or flukes, and propel themselves by powerful up-and-down movements of their tail. Many small marine animals simply drift with the current, but jellyfish move positively by opening and shutting their umbrella-like body. Octopuses and squids use the same technique, but squirt the water out through a narrow nozzle, jet-propelling themselves to safety.

WALRUSES   PULL THEMSELVES ACROSS ICE WITH THEIR TEETH

NAMES IN NATURE

Most people interested in natural history find the number of plants or animals illustrated in field guides bewildering, partly because there are so many, arranged in what may appear to be quite a random manner, but mostly because most guides cover areas as large as a continent, containing many wild plants or animals we may never see.

What is a "Species"?

Chaffinches and goldfinches are obviously related to each other as finches. They have similar beaks, feet and habits, but in the wild they never interbreed. Birdwatchers can recognize them as distinct from each other, and so can they. Several factors prevent interbreeding, and plumage is one of them. Chaffinches recognize the plumage colours and patterns only of other chaffinches when selecting mates. Courtship display reinforces this. Displaying male goldfinches mean nothing to female chaffinches. Ecological barriers also exist. Goldfinches are birds of heath and scrub, but chaffinches are mainly woodland birds, so the two rarely meet. So there are two distinct groups of birds which do not interbreed, for a variety of reasons, with other groups. Each of these groups is called a "species".

If species occur over wide geographical areas, then small local variations may occur in colour or voice. These local populations are called races or subspecies.

Evolution has ensured that each species is suited to its particular portion of a habitat, or niche. Any variants that occur are quickly eliminated, as they cannot compete well for food, living space, or breeding areas. If the niche changes, however, then one of these variants (plant or animal) may have a better chance of survival. This could mean that, in the course of time, a new species might develop.

Naming and Arranging

Birds known as robins in the USA are very different from the robins of Europe. Early colonists of America saw a red-breasted thrush and, out of nostalgia for home, they called it "robin". This sort of occurrence causes problems when we study birds (or other animals and plants) worldwide. To overcome this, each species has a scientific name derived from Latin, or Greek (or sometimes both), which is used everywhere in the world in books and field guides. Knowledge of these scientific names is very valuable to all naturalists who travel widely.

Researchers called taxonomists and systematists in museums throughout the world have worked out the relationships of living things, and have grouped them together. Some now use molecular biological techniques at the forefront of science, called genetic fingerprinting, to help establish relationships, because the fact that two animals or plants *look* similar may not indicate a real relationship. It may be that they have developed to survive in the same habitat, which is called parallel evolution. Because of their long curved wings, swifts and swallows look similar, but they are not related other than by being birds. The anatomical similarity is due to the fact that both have evolved to spend much of their lives on the wing feeding on insects.

Closely related species are placed in the same genus. Again using birds as an example, black terns

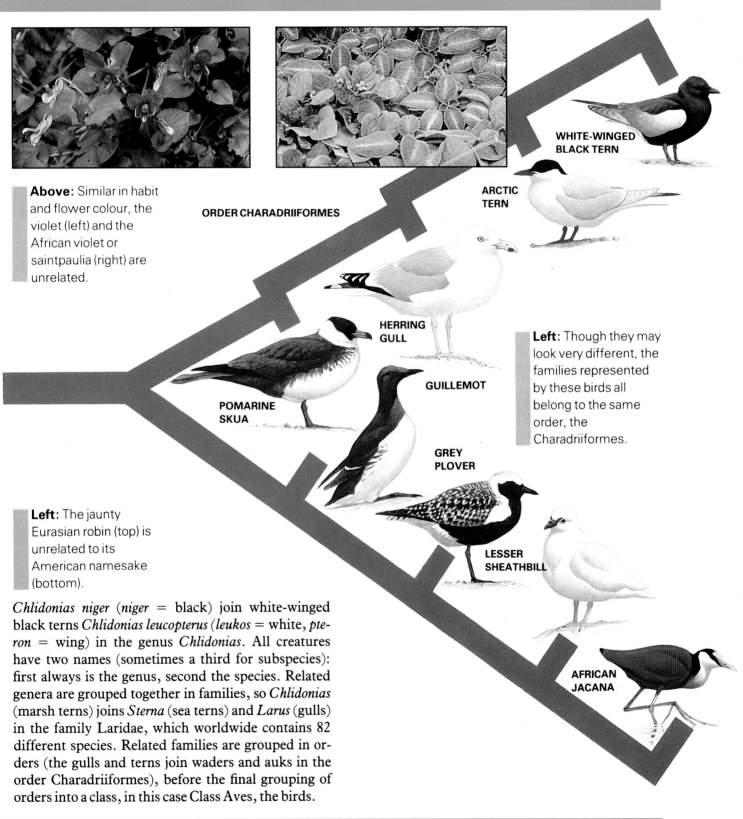

Above: Similar in habit and flower colour, the violet (left) and the African violet or saintpaulia (right) are unrelated.

ORDER CHARADRIIFORMES

WHITE-WINGED BLACK TERN

ARCTIC TERN

HERRING GULL

POMARINE SKUA

GUILLEMOT

Left: Though they may look very different, the families represented by these birds all belong to the same order, the Charadriiformes.

GREY PLOVER

LESSER SHEATHBILL

AFRICAN JACANA

Left: The jaunty Eurasian robin (top) is unrelated to its American namesake (bottom).

Chlidonias niger (*niger* = black) join white-winged black terns *Chlidonias leucopterus* (*leukos* = white, *pteron* = wing) in the genus *Chlidonias*. All creatures have two names (sometimes a third for subspecies): first always is the genus, second the species. Related genera are grouped together in families, so *Chlidonias* (marsh terns) joins *Sterna* (sea terns) and *Larus* (gulls) in the family Laridae, which worldwide contains 82 different species. Related families are grouped in orders (the gulls and terns join waders and auks in the order Charadriiformes), before the final grouping of orders into a class, in this case Class Aves, the birds.

THE GREEN WOODPECKER HAS 30 POPULAR NAMES, INCLUDING RAINBIRD AND YAFFLE

WILDLIFE AT RISK

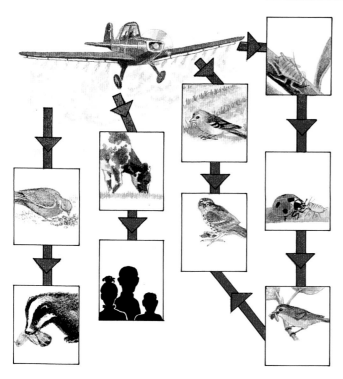

Almost everywhere around the globe, wildlife is at risk, and the pressures are increasing daily. Sometimes the threats are deliberate, like the huge-scale commercial felling of rainforests. Harvesting valuable timber trees would be acceptable if foresters replanted the trees extracted by loggers, but this rarely happens.

Besides their value as wildlife habitats, major forests have another important global function. As they grow, they use up huge amounts of atmospheric carbon dioxide (CO_2), locking it up in their leaves and timber. This helps reduce the "greenhouse effect" caused by excessive levels of CO_2 and other gases, which is leading to a warming of the earth's climate.

Gases

Much atmospheric CO_2 comes from power stations, homes and vehicles burning fossil fuels such as coal and oil. These are non-renewable resources: once burnt, there are no more, and stocks may last only another century. We must remember that *we* all expect electric light and heating to be available at the flick of a switch, and to travel where we want, which creates the demand for fuel. Burning coal or oil releases other gases besides CO_2, including sulphur oxides, which may be a major component of acid rain,

which threatens to kill vast areas of forest. The alternative is to use nuclear power stations, but, despite massive safety features, disastrous accidents happen with disturbing frequency. Loss of human, plant and animal life, and unknown genetic effects of mutations caused by radiation, make this a frightening option.

Oil

Oil is transported by sea, and risks of devastating pollution following shipwrecks are high. Wildlife losses can be enormous, including many seabirds and the rare sea otter. Detergents used to clear oil slicks damage plankton more than oil itself does. Thor Heyerdahl, exploring the South Atlantic on his raft *Ra*, found oil pollution far from shipping lanes. This originates from ships cleaning out fuel tanks at sea. Conservation bodies have protested about oil pollution for almost a century. Surely the time has come for international action to impose massive fines and imprisonment to end this unnecessary pollution for ever.

Pesticides

Farmers have relied heavily on poisonous chemicals to kill pests. DDT was an extremely effective pesticide, developed during the 1940s, cheap to make, easy and apparently safe to use. Millions of lives were saved using DDT to kill the mosquitoes carrying the tropical disease malaria. Only when peregrine falcon numbers dropped alarmingly was it realized that DDT was not so safe. It accumulates in animals' body fats, in the case of peregrines interfering with their breeding ability and causing them to lay thin-shelled, easily-

Above: Poisons such as pesticides can reach every part of the web of life.

Right: Waterways are the natural collecting points for pollution from many sources.

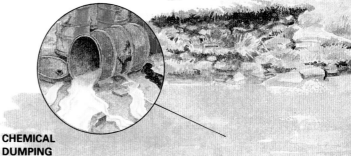

CHEMICAL DUMPING

broken eggs. DDT was banned, and much safer pesticide-testing has been introduced. Biological control now replaces pesticides to combat pests and diseases by encouraging their *natural* enemies – and peregrine populations have returned to normal levels.

Habitat Destruction

Greatest of all threats is building. Industrialists see the world's wild places such as estuaries as waste land, ideal for building. Remote beautiful coasts in warm countries are being "opened up" for tourism. Irreplaceable marshes are destroyed in case mosquitoes breed in them, and sand dunes vanish under hotels.

Many problems arise from *our* desire to make "progress", to lead healthier lives in comfortable surroundings, to travel on holiday, or to combat starvation in poor countries. Our problem is balancing our needs and interests with those of the other animals and plants that share our planet.

Above: Destruction of the forests threatens the tree species involved, and causes soil erosion.

AGRICULTURAL PESTICIDES

DOMESTIC REFUSE

INDUSTRIAL BY-PRODUCTS

URBAN DRAINAGE

EVERY YEAR, RAINFOREST EQUAL IN AREA TO SWITZERLAND FELLED

CONSERVATION

Man is continually advancing into the diminishing natural regions of the world and developing the land. So it is essential to set aside substantial areas of natural vegetation so that the plants and animals of a particular habitat can live on undisturbed. This is important to mankind, too, because in the complicated web of life all living things depend in some way on each other.

Choosing Nature Reserves

Nature reserves are chosen for many reasons. In countries with high populations, many towns and intensive farmland, they serve as reservoirs, releasing plants and animals to enrich the surrounding regions. Some are living museums, preserving the last remnants of a plant or animal species.

Lake Nakuru in Kenya is a spectacular example. Here millions of lesser flamingoes feed on the microscopic algae that flourish in the highly alkaline water. But even they are threatened. A copper-processing plant is being built nearby, and factory waste containing copper would poison the essential algae if it drained into the lake. Even in nature reserves, plant and animal populations may need to be kept under control. For example, although African elephants are a threatened species, in some reserves their numbers are increasing so fast that they are causing extensive habitat destruction as hungry herds roam in search of food, uprooting trees and bushes as they go. In such circumstances it may sadly be necessary to shoot some older and sick animals to restore the balance.

AVOCET

BELL HEATHER

Above: Nature reserves protect large areas of threatened habitats from encroaching urban, industrial or farming development, and allow rare plants and animals to flourish in peace.

Left: Extinction threatens as numbers of all rhinoceros species are at an all-time low.

INTERNATIONAL ORGANIZATIONS: WWF – WORLD-WIDE FUND FOR NATURE

MARSH HARRIER

WHAT CAN BE DONE?

By joining one, or better several, local, national or international conservation societies you assist them in several ways. The larger their membership grows, the more power they have as our "watchdogs" when advising or opposing governments or industrialists, and the more reserves they can afford to buy and protect. Practical support, assisting in local or nationwide censuses or studies, is equally valuable and helps provide the facts on which conservation planning must be based.

Creative Management

Ecologists may also work to recreate lost habitats. Minsmere in eastern England is an excellent example of environmental engineering, where lakes have been dug and islands moulded and planted up to replace wetland habitat destroyed two centuries ago. Species approaching extinction can be taken into captivity for specially planned breeding programmes. Néné, or Hawaiian geese, have been brought back from the verge of extinction in captive-breeding programmes founded by the late Sir Peter Scott, and now sufficient birds are available for many to be returned to recolonize their former haunts in the Hawaiian islands.

Persecution Persists

Sadly, human persecution of wild animals continues in many countries, where shooting for sport is a common weekend pastime with few restrictions. There are many rare plants threatened by the indiscriminate collectors wishing to introduce them as exotic greenhouse orchids or as humbler garden cyclamens or tulips.

In Africa and Asia, all five species of rhinoceros are endangered, threatened by poachers, and four of the five are now extremely rare. Poachers shoot, poison or snare the rhinos and then only cut off the horn. In many parts of the world this is supposed, against all the evidence, to have almost magical medicinal powers. Many skilled wardens are needed to combat this dreadful trade, but it involves danger and requires guns and helicopters; this policing is very expensive.

IUCN – INTERNATIONAL UNION FOR CONSERVATION OF NATURE AND NATURAL RESOURCES